QUESTION YOUR TRUTH OF THOUGHTS

QUESTION YOUR TRUTH OF THOUGHTS

HOW YOUR MINDSET CAN START AND STOP YOUR SUFFERING

THOUGHT TRANSFORMATION
BOOK 1

JAMES CONANT

Copyright © 2024 by James Conant

All rights reserved. No part of this book may be reproduced, stored in a retrieval system, or transmitted in any form or by any means, electronic, mechanical, photocopying, recording, or otherwise, without the prior written permission of the publisher, Book Bound Studios.

The information contained in this book is based on the author's personal experiences and research. While every effort has been made to ensure the accuracy of the information presented, the author and publisher cannot be held responsible for any errors or omissions.

This book is intended for general informational purposes only and is not a substitute for professional medical, legal, or financial advice. If you have specific questions about any medical, legal, or financial matters, you should consult with a qualified healthcare professional, attorney, or financial advisor.

Book Bound Studios is not affiliated with any product or vendor mentioned in this book. The views expressed in this book are those of the author and do not necessarily reflect the views of Book Bound Studios.

Dedicated to all who weather life's storms. May you find strength, resilience, and transformation within these pages.

Out of suffering have emerged the strongest souls;
the most massive characters are seared with scars.

— KAHLIL GIBRAN

CONTENTS

The Journey Begins   xiii

1. THE NATURE OF SUFFERING   1
   Defining Suffering   1
   Historical Perspectives   3
   Suffering in Modern Times   5
   The Universality of Suffering   7
   Personal Stories of Suffering   9
   The Purpose of Suffering   11
   Chapter Summary   13

2. MINDSET MATTERS   15
   Fixed vs. Growth Mindset   15
   The Power of Belief   17
   Shaping Your Reality   19
   Cultivating a Positive Mindset   21
   Mindset Shifts for Overcoming Suffering   23
   Chapter Summary   25

3. THE ROLE OF EMOTIONS   27
   Understanding Emotions   27
   Emotions and Suffering   29
   Managing Emotional Pain   31
   The Power of Empathy   33
   Transforming Emotions   35
   Chapter Summary   37

4. COPING MECHANISMS   39
   Healthy vs. Unhealthy Coping   39
   Building Resilience   41
   Mindfulness and Meditation   43
   The Role of Community   45

Finding Meaning in Suffering 47
Self-Care Strategies 49
Chapter Summary 51

5. THE POWER OF RELATIONSHIPS 53
Social Support Systems 53
The Impact of Loneliness 55
Building Meaningful Connections 57
Relationships and Healing 59
Navigating Conflict 62
The Role of Love and Compassion 64
Chapter Summary 66

6. OVERCOMING OBSTACLES 69
Identifying Obstacles 69
The Role of Perseverance 71
Learning from Failure 73
Adaptability and Change 74
Setting and Achieving Goals 76
The Power of Persistence 78
Chapter Summary 80

7. THE SEARCH FOR MEANING 83
What is Meaning? 83
Finding Purpose 85
The Role of Faith and Spirituality 88
Meaning Through Work 90
Contributing to Others 92
Chapter Summary 94

8. THE BODY-MIND CONNECTION 97
Physical Health and Mental Well-being 97
The Impact of Nutrition 99
Exercise and Mental Health 101
Sleep and Recovery 103
Stress Management 105
Chapter Summary 107

9. **THE SCIENCE OF HAPPINESS**   109
    Understanding Happiness   109
    Psychology of Happiness   111
    Happiness and Health   113
    Cultivating Joy   115
    The Role of Gratitude   117
    Sustainable Happiness   119
    Chapter Summary   121

10. **RESILIENCE IN THE FACE OF ADVERSITY**   123
    What is Resilience?   123
    Building Resilience   125
    Resilience in Action   127
    Overcoming Trauma   129
    The Role of Forgiveness   131
    Chapter Summary   133

11. **THE ART OF LETTING GO**   135
    Understanding Attachment   135
    The Process of Letting Go   137
    Forgiveness and Release   139
    Embracing Change   141
    Living in the Present   143
    Chapter Summary   145

12. **CREATING YOUR PATH**   147
    Vision for the Future   147
    Setting Intentions   149
    Taking Action   151
    The Importance of Patience   154
    Celebrating Progress   156
    Continuous Growth   158
    Chapter Summary   160

    The Journey Continues   163

Your Feedback Matters 169
About the Author 171

THE JOURNEY BEGINS

Understanding Mindset

Mindset, a seemingly simple word, holds the power to shape our perception of suffering and our journey through it. It's the lens through which we view our experiences, the filter that colors our reality. But understanding this concept is more than acknowledging its existence; it's about diving deep into how it influences every aspect of our lives, especially when navigating the turbulent waters of suffering.

Now, understanding mindset is the first step on this journey to *"Question Your Truth of Thoughts."* It's about recognizing that our thoughts, attitudes, and beliefs about suffering profoundly impact our ability to cope with it. It's

The Journey Begins

acknowledging that while we may not have control over the external events that cause us pain, we do have control over how we interpret and respond to them.

As we delve deeper into this topic, we'll explore the different types of mindsets and how they influence our experience of suffering. We'll look at the fixed mindset, which sees challenges as permanent and impossible, and the growth mindset, which views suffering as a temporary state and an opportunity for personal development. We'll also discuss strategies for cultivating a more adaptive and resilient mindset that can help us navigate the complexities of suffering with grace and strength.

So, as we embark on this journey together, I invite you to reflect on your mindset. Consider how it has shaped your experiences of suffering in the past and how it might influence your path forward. Remember, the goal is not to eliminate suffering from our lives—that's an impossible task—but to learn how to move through it with purpose, growth, and hope.

The Role of Suffering

Suffering, in its many forms, is a universal part of the human experience. It's a concept that binds us. Yet, how we perceive and interact with our suffering can profoundly influence our journey through life. It's not just about the pain or the hardship itself, but how we frame it within our minds that genuinely shapes our path.

At first glance, suffering seems like an unwelcome intruder, something to be avoided at all costs. But if we shift our perspective slightly, we can see it as a powerful teacher, a catalyst for growth and transformation. This is not to romanticize pain or suggest that we should seek it out, but rather to acknowledge that when suffering does enter our lives, it also brings with it the opportunity to learn, adapt, and evolve.

Consider the concept of resilience. It's a quality that we admire, a strength that we aspire to. Yet resilience is not born from a life of ease and comfort. It is forged in the fire of adversity. Each challenge, setback, and moment of suffering has the potential to build our resilience and teach us about our own strength and determination.

Moreover, suffering can deepen our empathy and connect us more profoundly to others. It's a reminder of our shared humanity. This bridge links our experiences to the collective story of human struggle and perseverance. When we understand our own suffering, we are better equipped to understand the suffering of others, to offer compassion, and to support those around us.

But how do we make this shift in perspective? How do we move from viewing suffering as a purely negative force to recognizing its potential for positive growth? It starts with mindset. Our mindset is the lens through which we

The Journey Begins

view the world, the narrative we tell ourselves about what happens to us. We can transform our relationship with suffering by cultivating a mindset that embraces growth and sees challenges as opportunities.

This transformation doesn't happen overnight. It requires patience, practice, and perseverance. It's a journey that may be fraught with difficulty but also rich with rewards. As we navigate this path, we learn about suffering and ourselves. We discover our capacity for resilience, empathy, and growth. And in doing so, we find that suffering, while an inevitable part of life, does not have to define us. Instead, it can be a stepping stone, a part of our journey toward becoming more resilient, empathetic, and understanding individuals.

Setting the Stage

Imagine standing at the edge of a vast forest. The dense and towering trees stretch into the horizon, their tops lost to the sky. With its unknown paths and hidden depths, this forest is much like the journey of understanding mindset and suffering. It's vast, sometimes daunting, but filled with insights and revelations waiting to be discovered. As we set the stage for this exploration, we must acknowledge the ground we stand on and the tools at our disposal.

Mindset and suffering are intertwined in complex and deeply personal ways. Our mindset, the lens through which we view the world, shapes our experiences, reactions, and, ultimately, our reality. It's the foundation of our thoughts, beliefs, and attitudes. Suffering, on the other hand, is an inevitable part of the human experience. It's a universal truth that touches every life, yet it's experienced uniquely by each of us. The relationship between mindset and suffering is not just about how suffering affects our mindset but also how our mindset can transform our experience of suffering.

As we embark on this journey, it's essential to approach with an open mind and a willing heart. The path will be challenging. There will be moments of discomfort, perhaps even pain, as we confront truths about ourselves and the nature of suffering. However, there will also be profound insight, beauty, and transformation moments. The journey through the forest of mindset and suffering is as much about discovery as recovery.

This section prepares us for the journey ahead. We're gathering our tools, mapping our route, and bracing ourselves for the challenges and rewards. It's an invitation to look inward, question, and grow. As we delve deeper into understanding mindset and the role of suffering, remember that every step is a step toward greater understanding and, ultimately, liberation.

So, take a deep breath. The journey begins here, at the forest's edge, with the first step into the unknown. Together, we'll navigate the complexities of mindset and suffering, seeking light in the shadows and strength in the struggles. The path may be long and, at times, arduous, but the journey promises to be one of the most meaningful and transformative of our lives.

How to Use This Book

When you embark on a journey through the pages of this book, you're not just reading; you're stepping into a process of transformation. This isn't a passive experience. It's interactive, reflective, and, most importantly, practical. To get the most out of this exploration into mindset and suffering, consider this section as your roadmap, guiding you on navigating these pages effectively.

First and foremost, keep an open mind. The concepts and strategies discussed here may challenge your beliefs about suffering and the power of mindset. That's okay. Growth often begins at the edge of our comfort zones. As you encounter new ideas, approach them with curiosity rather than resistance. Ask yourself how these insights can apply to your life, even if they seem counterintuitive at first glance.

Reflective practice is critical. At the end of each section, you'll find a chapter summary, designed to reinforce the ideas mentioned in the topic. Take advantage of these. Expand on them, or even write your own. The real magic happens when you take the time to reflect on your experiences and perceptions.

Dialogue is another crucial element of this journey. While this book serves as your guide, your insights and experiences are what genuinely enrich the process. Share your thoughts, questions, and discoveries with others. Discussing these concepts with friends, family, or fellow readers online can open up new perspectives and deepen your understanding.

Remember, there's no right or wrong way to use this book. Some may read it from cover to cover, while others might jump to sections that resonate most with their current challenges. Both approaches are valid. What matters most is your engagement with the material and your willingness to apply it to your life.

Finally, be patient with yourself. Changing deeply ingrained mindsets and understanding the role of suffering in personal growth is a process, not a one-time event. There will be moments of insight and clarity, as well as times of doubt and confusion, which are all part of the journey. Keep moving forward, and trust that each step, no matter how small, is moving you closer to a deeper understanding of yourself and the transformative power of your mindset.

As we embark on this journey together, remember that this book is more than just a collection of pages. It's a companion to understanding the intricate dance between

The Journey Begins

mindset and suffering. Use it well, and let the journey begin.

Invitation to You, the Reader

Welcome, dear reader. You're about to embark on a journey that's as challenging as it is rewarding. This book isn't just a collection of pages; it's an invitation to explore the depths of your mindset, and the role suffering plays in shaping it. If you've picked up this book, chances are you're no stranger to hardship. Maybe you're struggling, searching for a beacon of hope, or curious about the intricate dance between our mental states and trials.

I want you to know that this book is for you. It's for anyone who's ever felt the world's weight on their shoulders and wondered if there's a way to lighten the load. It's for the seekers of wisdom who understand that suffering. At the same time, an inevitable part of life doesn't have to define us.

As we journey through these pages together, I invite you to keep an open mind. Some ideas may challenge your current beliefs, while others may seem like familiar friends. Either way, I encourage you to approach this book as a reader and an active participant in your journey of self-discovery.

Remember, this isn't about finding quick fixes or easy answers. It's about embarking on a path of understanding, acceptance, and transformation. So, please take a deep breath, turn the page, and let's begin this journey together. Your mindset and how you navigate suffering are about to change in ways you might never have imagined. Welcome aboard.

1

THE NATURE OF SUFFERING

Defining Suffering

At the heart of our exploration into the nature of suffering lies a fundamental question: What exactly is suffering? It's a widely used and profoundly personal term, often evoking various emotions and responses. To understand suffering, we must first acknowledge its multifaceted nature. It's not just physical pain, nor is it solely emotional distress. Instead, suffering encompasses a broad spectrum of experiences, from the acute sting of a physical injury to the profound depths of grief and despair.

Suffering is universal yet uniquely individual. What one person experiences as a minor inconvenience, another might perceive as an insurmountable obstacle. This subjective nature of suffering makes it a complex phenomenon to define. However, at its core, suffering signals something significant is amiss—either in our bodies, minds, or environment. It acts as a messenger, albeit unwelcome, alerting us to pay attention and, ideally, to take action.

But why focus on suffering? Understanding suffering is crucial because it's integral to the human condition. It shapes our experiences, influences our decisions, and can even alter the course of our lives. By examining suffering, we gain insights into resilience, empathy, and the human capacity for change. It teaches us about our limits and strengths, pushing us to explore new avenues for growth and healing.

Moreover, our response to suffering—our own and others—reveals much about our values, beliefs, and character. It can bring out the best in us, fostering compassion, solidarity, and a desire to alleviate pain. Conversely, it can challenge us, testing our patience, endurance, and, sometimes, our sense of self.

In this section, we'll delve deeper into the nature of suffering, exploring its causes, its effects, and, most importantly, how our mindset plays a crucial role in navigating the turbulent waters of distress. By understanding suffering, we equip ourselves with the knowledge to face it head-on, learn from it, and ultimately find a path through it.

Historical Perspectives

Throughout history, suffering has been a central theme in the human experience, profoundly shaping philosophies, religions, and individual mindsets. Let's take a moment to journey back and explore how different cultures and thinkers have grappled with the nature of suffering, offering relevant insights.

In ancient times, the Greeks viewed suffering as an inevitable part of life, a theme deeply embedded in their mythology and tragedies. The story of Sisyphus, condemned to roll a boulder up a hill only for it to roll back down each time, symbolizes the endless cycle of suffering and the human condition's inherent struggle. This perspective teaches us about accepting life's challenges and the resilience of the human spirit.

Moving East, Buddhism offers a unique lens on suffering. The First Noble Truth, "Life is suffering," is not a pessimistic view but a straightforward acknowledgment of life's inherent difficulties. The Buddha's teachings emphasize that suffering arises from attachment, and we can navigate a path toward liberation and peace by understanding the nature of our desires. This perspective invites us to reflect on our attachments and their role in our suffering.

In the Middle Ages, Christian theologians like Augustine and Thomas Aquinas pondered suffering within the context of sin and divine providence. They argued that suffering could lead to spiritual growth and closer union with God, offering a redemptive view of suffering. This idea of suffering as a pathway to spiritual enlightenment and redemption has influenced countless individuals' personal journeys of faith and resilience.

Fast-forward to the modern era, existential philosophers such as Friedrich Nietzsche and Jean-Paul Sartre explored suffering through the lens of human freedom and the search for meaning. Nietzsche's famous proclamation, "What does not kill me, makes me stronger," captures the essence of finding strength and purpose through adversity. These thinkers challenge us to confront our suffering head-on and to derive personal meaning and growth from our struggles.

As we reflect on these historical perspectives, it becomes clear that suffering is a complex and multifaceted concept deeply intertwined with the human condition. Each cultural and philosophical viewpoint offers a different path for understanding and navigating suffering, whether through acceptance, spiritual growth, detachment, or the search for meaning.

What's fascinating is how these ancient insights still resonate with us today, offering valuable lessons on resilience, acceptance, and the pursuit of peace amidst life's inevitable challenges. As we continue our exploration of the nature of suffering, let's keep these historical perspectives in mind, drawing on the wisdom of the past to inform our understanding and approach to suffering in the present.

Suffering in Modern Times

In today's fast-paced world, suffering takes on new forms, often masked by the hustle and bustle of modern life. While the nature of suffering has evolved, its impact on the human psyche remains profound. With its constant connectivity and the pressure to keep up, the digital age has introduced a unique set of challenges that contribute to modern suffering. This section delves into how these contemporary issues influence our mindset and contribute to our suffering.

The advent of social media, for instance, has brought about a comparison culture where individuals measure their self-worth against the curated lives of others. This constant comparison can lead to feelings of inadequacy, loneliness, and suffering. The irony is palpable; individuals feel more isolated in a world more connected than ever. The pressure to present a perfect life online can exacerbate feelings of not being good enough, leading to a cycle of suffering that is hard to break.

Moreover, the modern workplace, emphasizing productivity and success, contributes to this cycle of suffering. The fear of not meeting expectations or achieving one's goals can lead to stress, anxiety, and burnout. This relentless pursuit of success, often at the expense of personal well-being, highlights a skewed mindset where self-worth is tied to professional achievements.

However, it's not all doom and gloom. Recognizing the sources of modern suffering is the first step toward addressing them. We can shift our mindset by understanding that much of our suffering is rooted in societal expectations and perceptions. It's about redefining what success means personally and finding value in the journey, not just the destination.

Mindfulness and self-compassion emerge as powerful tools in combating modern suffering. By being present and kind to ourselves, we can navigate the challenges of modern life with a sense of peace and resilience. It's about accepting that suffering is a part of life but doesn't have to define us. We can change our relationship with suffering, transforming it into an opportunity for growth and self-discovery.

In conclusion, suffering in modern times is shaped by the complexities of the digital age and societal pressures. However, by adopting a mindset of mindfulness and self-compassion, we can mitigate its impact on our lives. It's a journey of self-discovery, where we learn to embrace our imperfections and find joy in the simple moments. By doing so, we can navigate the modern world with purpose and well-being, turning our suffering into a source of strength.

The Universality of Suffering

At the heart of human experience lies a truth as old as time: suffering is universal. It's a thread that weaves through the fabric of every life, regardless of age, background, or circumstance. This isn't a pessimistic view but a realistic acknowledgment of the human condition. Understanding this universality can be the first step toward a profound transformation in how we perceive our struggles and the struggles of others.

Imagine, for a moment, walking down a busy street. Each person you pass carries their own set of challenges, fears, and pains, invisible to the casual observer. Some may be grappling with loss, others with illness, and yet others with deep-seated fears or insecurities. The specifics vary infinitely, but the underlying reality of suffering does not. It's a common denominator, a shared aspect of existence that transcends individual differences.

Recognizing the universality of suffering serves a dual purpose. First, it fosters empathy and connection. When we realize that everyone around us is fighting their own battles, just as we are, it becomes easier to extend kindness and understanding. This empathy doesn't erase suffering, but it can make the burden a little lighter for ourselves and others.

Secondly, this recognition can be incredibly liberating. It helps us understand that suffering is not a sign of personal failure or a punishment for our mistakes. Instead, it's part of the very nature of being alive. This perspective can free us from the added layers of guilt or shame we often heap upon ourselves when faced with difficulties. It allows us to approach our suffering with a sense of acceptance and, from there, seek paths toward healing or growth.

Of course, acknowledging the universality of suffering is just the beginning. It only provides some of the answers or solves all the problems. What it does do, however, is open the door to a more compassionate, empathetic, and realistic approach to dealing with life's inevitable challenges. It reminds us that we're not alone in our struggles, and in that shared experience, there's a kind of comfort and strength to be found.

As we move forward, let's remember this: suffering might be universal, but so are the capacities for resilience, compassion, and growth. By embracing the former, we unlock the potential for the latter, not just in ourselves but in our collective journey through life.

Personal Stories of Suffering

In the heart of every person lies a story of suffering. It's a universal experience, threading through the fabric of humanity, connecting us in our shared vulnerabilities. Yet, each story is profoundly unique, painting a vivid picture of struggle, resilience, and sometimes, transformation. Let's delve into a few personal stories illuminating the diverse landscapes of suffering and the indomitable spirit of the human soul.

Anna, a middle-aged teacher, found herself engulfed in the depths of despair following the sudden loss of her husband. The world as she knew it crumbled overnight, leaving her to navigate a labyrinth of grief and loneliness. Her suffering was not just emotional but also physical, manifesting in sleepless nights and a pervasive sense of fatigue that seemed to color her every waking moment. Yet, through her journey, Anna discovered a wellspring of inner strength. She began to channel her pain into writing, transforming her grief into a series of poignant poems that spoke to the heart of loss and healing. She found solace and connection in sharing her work, reminding us that light can emerge from within, even in our darkest hours.

Then there's Michael, a young veteran whose body returned from war, but his mind remained on the battlefield. The physical scars were visible, but the invisible wounds cut the deepest. Plagued by nightmares and a constant state of hyper-vigilance, Michael's suffering was a silent battle fought in the shadows of his own psyche. It was in the companionship of a service dog named Max that Michael found his lifeline. Max's unwavering presence provided a sense of security and understanding that words could not. Together, they embarked on a healing journey, a testament to the power of non-verbal communication and the healing potential of unconditional love.

Lastly, we meet Priya, who faced the debilitating grip of depression. For Priya, suffering was a thick fog that clouded her vision, making the simplest tasks seem impossible. The world lost its color, and joy became a distant memory. Yet, it was through reaching out for help and embracing the slow, often frustrating, process of therapy that Priya began to see glimmers of light. She learned to navigate her mental landscape with compassion, recognizing that healing is not linear but a series of small victories and setbacks. Priya's story reminds us that sometimes, the bravest thing we can do is ask for help; in doing so, we open the door to recovery.

These stories, each unique in their contours of suffering, share a common thread—the resilience of the human spirit. They remind us that suffering, while an inevitable part of the human experience, also holds the potential for growth, connection, and profound transformation. As we journey through our own landscapes of pain, let these stories serve as beacons of hope, illuminating the path toward healing and reminding us that we are not alone.

The Purpose of Suffering

In exploring the purpose of suffering, it's crucial to acknowledge that it is a universal human experience in its myriad forms. It's a thread that weaves through the fabric of every life, regardless of age, background, or circumstance. But why? Why is suffering such a pervasive part of our existence?

At first glance, suffering seems like an unwelcome intruder, something to be avoided at all costs. Yet, when we delve deeper, we uncover that suffering has the potential to serve a profound purpose in our lives. It can act as a catalyst for growth, transformation, and a deeper understanding of both ourselves and the world around us.

Consider, for a moment, the concept of resilience. It's a quality admired and aspired to, but rarely is it understood that resilience is often forged in the fires of suffering. We develop the strength and flexibility to handle future adversities through facing and overcoming challenges. This doesn't mean we seek out suffering or glorify it; instead, we recognize its role in shaping our character and capabilities.

On a personal note, I recall a period of intense

difficulty in my own life. It was a time when everything that could go wrong did, leaving me feeling defeated and alone. Yet, it was also during this time that I discovered my strength and the depth of my resilience. This experience, as painful as it was, taught me invaluable lessons about perseverance, hope, and the importance of seeking support when needed. It was a stark reminder that sometimes, our greatest trials lead to our most significant growth.

Suffering also has the unique ability to deepen our empathy and connect us with others. It's through our own experiences of pain that we can truly understand and share in the suffering of others. This shared vulnerability binds us together, fostering community and mutual support. It reminds us that we are not alone in our struggles and that there is strength in solidarity.

Furthermore, suffering can prompt us to question and seek meaning. It challenges us to look beyond the surface and explore what truly matters. For many, this journey of introspection leads to a greater appreciation for life's blessings and a renewed focus on personal values and priorities.

In conclusion, while suffering is an inevitable part of life, it's not without purpose. It has the power to teach, transform, and connect us in ways that comfort and ease never could. By embracing its lessons, we can emerge from our trials with a deeper understanding of ourselves, a strengthened resolve, and a greater capacity for compassion. Remember, it's not the suffering that defines us but how we respond.

Chapter Summary

- Suffering is a complex, multifaceted experience encompassing physical pain and emotional distress, signaling that something significant is amiss in our bodies, minds, or environment.
- It is both universal and uniquely individual, with its subjective nature making it a complex phenomenon to define. Yet, it plays a crucial role in shaping human experiences and decisions.
- Historical perspectives on suffering, from ancient Greek mythology to Buddhism and modern existential philosophy, highlight its central role in human life and offer various paths for understanding and navigating it.
- In modern times, suffering has evolved with societal pressures and the digital age, with social media and workplace stress contributing to feelings of inadequacy, loneliness, and burnout.
- Mindfulness and self-compassion are powerful tools for combating modern suffering. They

emphasize the importance of redefining personal success and finding value in life's journey.
- The universality of suffering fosters empathy and connection among people, reminding us that suffering is not a sign of personal failure but a part of the human condition.
- Personal stories of suffering, such as those of Anna, Michael, and Priya, illustrate the diverse landscapes of suffering and the resilience of the human spirit in facing challenges and finding growth and transformation.
- The purpose of suffering is explored as a catalyst for growth, transformation, and deeper understanding, with resilience, empathy, and the search for meaning highlighted as critical lessons learned from facing and overcoming challenges.

2
MINDSET MATTERS

Fixed vs. Growth Mindset

When we talk about mindset, we're diving into the very core of how we perceive our abilities and challenges. It's like looking through a lens that colors our entire world. On one side, we have the fixed mindset. This belief system suggests our talents, intelligence, and abilities are carved in stone. "You've got what you're born with," it whispers, and that's that. It's a perspective that can make suffering feel like a dead end, a permanent state that defines us.

On the flip side, there's the growth mindset, a term popularized by psychologist Carol Dweck. This is the belief that our abilities can be developed through dedication and hard work. It's an understanding that brains and talent are just the starting point. This perspective sees suffering not as a defining moment but as a stepping stone, an opportunity for growth and learning.

Imagine two climbers facing a steep and daunting mountain. The one with a fixed mindset looks up and thinks, "I either can climb it, or I can't. There's no point in trying if I'm going to fail." This mindset returns at the first sign of difficulty, viewing it as proof of their limitations.

However, the climber with a growth mindset sees the mountain and thinks, "This is going to be tough, but with effort, I can get better and eventually make it to the top." They understand that each attempt and failure is a chance to learn and improve. When they fall, they get back up, dust themselves off, and try again, each time a little wiser.

Now, let's return to suffering. In the throes of hardship, a fixed mindset can make us feel trapped. We might think, "This is just how things are. I can't change it." This mindset can lead to despair and resignation because it tells us our suffering is a fixed part of our identity.

Conversely, a growth mindset encourages resilience in the face of suffering. It tells us, "This is tough, but I can learn from it. I can grow stronger." It doesn't diminish the pain or the challenge but reframes it as an opportunity for development. With a growth mindset, suffering becomes a part of our journey, not the end of the road.

So, why does this matter? Because the mindset we adopt profoundly impacts how we navigate life's inevitable challenges and sufferings. It influences whether we see obstacles as impossible or as opportunities to evolve. It shapes our resilience, capacity to bounce back, and ability to find meaning and joy even in the darkest times.

As we move forward, remember that our mindset is not fixed. Just as we can develop our abilities, we can also cultivate a growth mindset. This choice can transform our relationship with suffering and lead us toward a path of growth, learning, and resilience.

The Power of Belief

Belief is a powerful tool. It shapes our thoughts, drives our actions, and, ultimately, molds our reality. In the context of mindset and suffering, the power of belief cannot be overstated. It's the bridge between enduring hardship and emerging stronger on the other side. Let's dive into how this works.

Imagine a similar scenario as before—two individuals facing the same challenge. One believes the challenge is impossible, a permanent fixture in one's life. The other sees it as a temporary obstacle, an opportunity for growth. Their beliefs about the situation will dictate their responses, resilience, and outcomes. This is where the distinction between a fixed and a growth mindset becomes crystal clear.

A fixed mindset convinces us that our abilities, intelligence, and coping capacity are static. We either have it or we don't. This belief system makes suffering feel like a dead end with no way out. It's a recipe for despair.

On the flip side, a growth mindset thrives when challenged. It views suffering as a part of the learning process, a stepping stone rather than a stumbling block. This doesn't mean those with a growth mindset don't feel pain or despair. They do. However, their belief that they can evolve through adversity fuels their resilience. It's a powerful testament to the human spirit's capacity to adapt and grow.

But how do we cultivate such a belief? It starts with self-awareness. The first step is to recognize our automatic thoughts in the face of suffering. These thoughts often stem from deep-seated beliefs about ourselves and the world. By challenging these beliefs, questioning their validity, and consciously choosing to adopt a more flexible and growth-oriented perspective, we begin to shift our mindset.

This shift doesn't happen overnight. It requires patience, practice, and persistence. It's about celebrating small victories, learning from setbacks, and understanding that progress is rarely linear. It's also about compassion—towards ourselves and others. It's crucial to recognize that everyone's journey with suffering is unique, and what works for one person may not work for another.

The power of belief in the context of mindset and suffering is profound. It can be the difference between feeling stuck in a perpetual cycle of despair and moving forward with hope and resilience. As we navigate our journeys, let's remember the transformative power of believing in our capacity to grow through what we go through. It's not just about surviving; it's about thriving.

Shaping Your Reality

It's not just about seeing the glass as half full or half empty; it's about understanding that it can be refilled. This perspective is crucial when navigating the complex interplay between mindset and suffering.

Consider, for a moment, the story of a young artist. This artist, much like anyone, faced their fair share of setbacks. Each rejection letter felt like a sharp jab to their confidence, each critique a heavy blow to their aspirations. It would have been easy, perhaps even understandable, for them to view these challenges as impossible, to see their dreams as unattainable. Yet, they chose a different path. They saw each rejection not as a failure but as a step closer to their goal, each critiquing a lesson to improve their craft. This shift in mindset transformed their journey, turning suffering into a catalyst for growth.

This anecdote mirrors a broader truth about the human experience. Our reality is shaped by the events that occur to us and our reactions to them. A fixed mindset that sees challenges as threats and failures as defining can turn suffering into a quagmire, trapping us in a cycle of despair. On the other hand, a growth mindset, which views challenges as opportunities and failures as lessons, can transform suffering into a stepping stone that propels us forward.

The power of belief plays a pivotal role in this process. Believing that we can learn from our suffering and emerge stronger and more resilient is the first step in reshaping our reality. It's about acknowledging our pain, understanding its source, and then taking action to move beyond it. This doesn't mean dismissing our suffering or pretending it doesn't exist. Instead, it's about changing our relationship with our struggles, viewing them through a lens of growth and potential.

In my own life, I've seen the truth of this principle time and again. A personal setback, which initially seemed like a devastating blow, became one of my most profound learning experiences. It was a difficult period, but embracing a growth mindset allowed me to reassess my priorities and grow in empathy and resilience. This experience, though painful, enriched my life in ways I could never have anticipated.

So, as we navigate the complexities of suffering, let us remember the power of our mindset. By adopting a growth mindset, we can transform our challenges into opportunities and our pain into progress. It's a journey that requires patience, resilience, and belief, but it can ultimately lead us to a richer, more fulfilling life.

Cultivating a Positive Mindset

In the journey of life, suffering is an inevitable companion. It's not the presence of suffering that defines our lives but how we respond to it. This is where the power of a positive mindset comes into play. Cultivating a positive mindset isn't about denying the reality of pain or hardship. Instead, it's about focusing on the potential for growth and learning that can emerge from our struggles.

Imagine you're planting a garden. You have a choice of seeds to sow: those of despair or those of hope. Planting seeds of despair will yield more suffering, but choosing seeds of hope can transform even the most barren soil into a place of life and growth. This metaphor illustrates the essence of cultivating a positive mindset. It's about consciously choosing to plant and nurture seeds of hope, resilience, and optimism in the garden of your mind.

But how do we cultivate such a mindset, especially when faced with the harsh realities of suffering? It starts with acknowledging our pain and allowing ourselves to feel it. Ignoring our suffering or pretending it doesn't exist only leads to more profound despair. Once we've acknowledged our suffering, we can look for the lessons it offers. Every challenge, every setback, and every heartache carries with it the potential for growth and learning.

Next, practice gratitude. It might seem counterintuitive to feel thankful while suffering, but gratitude can shift our focus from what we lack to what we have. This shift doesn't negate our pain but provides a broader perspective that includes the good in our lives alongside the challenges.

Another critical aspect of cultivating a positive mindset is to surround ourselves with positivity. This includes the people we spend time with, the media we consume, and the thoughts we entertain. Positivity breeds positivity, just as negativity breeds negativity. By consciously choosing positivity, we create an environment that nurtures our growth and resilience.

Finally, cultivating a positive mindset is a journey, not a destination. There will be days when positivity feels out of reach, and that's okay. What matters is that we continue to plant and nurture those seeds of hope, even when the soil feels barren. Over time, with patience and persistence, those seeds will take root and grow, transforming our experience of suffering and empowering us to live more fully and joyfully.

In essence, cultivating a positive mindset is about choosing how we respond to the suffering in our lives. It's a powerful tool that can transform our pain into a catalyst for growth, resilience, and a deeper appreciation for the beauty of life.

Mindset Shifts for Overcoming Suffering

Suffering seems to be an inevitable companion on the journey of life. Yet, how we face it and mold our experiences from it largely depends on our mindset. It's not just about seeing the glass as half full or half empty; it's about understanding that it can be refilled. This section delves into the transformative power of mindset shifts in overcoming suffering, drawing from psychological insights and personal experience.

Imagine navigating a labyrinth of train tracks, the path unclear and the destination uncertain. This is akin to the journey through suffering. However, with a map in hand, you can find your way out. This map represents our mindset. A shift in mindset doesn't erase the obstacles but illuminates paths we couldn't see before.

One pivotal mindset shift is moving from victimhood to agency. It's easy to feel like a victim of circumstances and that suffering is happening to us without our control. I remember feeling trapped by my circumstances, and my personal and professional life seemed to crumble simultaneously. It was a period of intense suffering. However, the moment I started to see myself as the navigator of my journey rather than a passenger, the situation began to change. This took time, and it was challenging. Still, the shift in perspective was the first step towards overcoming my suffering.

Another significant shift is embracing suffering as a teacher, not an enemy. It's about asking, "What can this experience teach me?" rather than "Why is this happening to me?" This approach doesn't diminish the pain or the challenge but allows us to extract wisdom and growth from our suffering. It's about finding meaning amid hardship, which can be a powerful catalyst for personal transformation.

Furthermore, cultivating gratitude in the face of suffering can profoundly alter our experience. This doesn't mean being thankful for the suffering itself but finding aspects of our life we can still be grateful for despite the suffering. It's about focusing on what we have, not what we've lost or what's causing us pain. This mindset shift can be a source of strength and resilience, offering us a lifeline in our darkest moments.

Lastly, fostering a mindset of openness and curiosity can transform our relationship with suffering. Instead of resisting or denying our pain, we can approach it with curiosity, asking ourselves what it reveals about our values, desires, and fears. This openness can lead to deeper self-awareness and, ultimately, to healing and growth.

In conclusion, while suffering is a universal aspect of the human experience, our mindset plays a crucial role in navigating it. By shifting our mindset from victimhood to agency, from seeing suffering as an enemy to a teacher, from despair to gratitude, and from resistance to openness, we can find our way through the busiest train tracks of our lives. These shifts don't promise an easy journey, but they offer us a way to emerge on the other side, intact and transformed.

Chapter Summary

- Mindset is crucial in how we perceive our abilities and challenges. A fixed mindset views talents as unchangeable, while a growth mindset believes in development through effort.
- A fixed mindset sees challenges and suffering as permanent and defining, leading to resignation. In contrast, a growth mindset views them as opportunities for learning and growth.
- The concept of mindset affects resilience. It influences whether we see obstacles as insurmountable or as chances to evolve, shaping our ability to bounce back and find joy in adversity.
- Cultivating a growth mindset involves recognizing and challenging our automatic thoughts and beliefs, embracing patience,

practice, and compassion towards ourselves and others.
- The power of belief bridges enduring hardship and emerging stronger. A growth mindset fosters resilience by viewing suffering as part of the learning process.
- Shaping our reality involves understanding that our reactions to events play a significant role, with a positive mindset focusing on potential growth from struggles.
- Cultivating a positive mindset involves acknowledging pain, practicing gratitude, surrounding ourselves with positivity, and understanding it's a journey with ups and downs.
- Mindset shifts, such as moving from victimhood to agency and seeing suffering as a teacher, can profoundly transform our relationship with suffering and lead to personal growth.

3

THE ROLE OF EMOTIONS

Understanding Emotions

Emotions are complex, multifaceted experiences that are crucial to our lives. They influence our decisions, shape our relationships, and affect our well-being. Understanding emotions, therefore, is about more than just recognizing when we're feeling happy or sad. It's about delving deeper into the intricate web of feelings that drive our thoughts and actions.

At the heart of it, emotions are our body's way of communicating with us. They signal when something is noteworthy, pleasant, dangerous, or undesirable. But here's the thing: emotions aren't just reactions to the world around us; they also shape our perception of that world. This means our emotional state can significantly influence how we interpret events, interact with others, and see ourselves.

Consider, for instance, the role of emotions in suffering. When we face challenges or hardships, our emotional responses can amplify our sense of suffering or help us navigate it. It's not just about feeling bad or good; it's about how those feelings guide our responses to adversity. Do they push us into a corner or spur us into action? This is where the power of mindset comes into play.

A mindset that embraces growth and resilience sees emotions not as obstacles but as signals. It's a perspective that encourages us to ask, "What is this emotion telling me?" rather than "Why do I have to feel this way?" This shift in questioning is subtle but profound. It moves us from passive suffering to active engagement with our emotional landscape.

Understanding our emotions also means recognizing their transient nature. Emotions come and go, often influenced by many factors, including our thoughts, physical states, and external circumstances. This realization can be liberating. It means that while we may not have control over the emotions we experience, we do have control over how we respond to them. We can choose to engage with our emotions in a way that supports our growth and well-being.

Moreover, understanding emotions is not just an

individual journey. It's also about empathy and connection. By recognizing and respecting the complexity of our own emotions, we become better equipped to understand and empathize with the emotions of others. This can lead to deeper, more meaningful relationships and a greater sense of connectedness.

Understanding emotions is a foundational aspect of navigating the landscape of mindset and suffering. It's about seeing emotions as messengers, teachers, and sometimes even as friends. By engaging with our emotions with curiosity and openness, we can uncover insights about ourselves and the world around us, paving the way for a more resilient and compassionate approach to life's challenges.

Emotions and Suffering

Emotions play a pivotal role in our experience of suffering. They are the lens through which we perceive and interpret our physical, emotional, or psychological pain. It's crucial to understand that emotions themselves are not the enemy; instead, our relationship with them can either exacerbate our suffering or lead us toward healing.

Consider for a moment the last time you felt a strong emotion, perhaps anger, sadness, or fear. These feelings, while uncomfortable, are inherently neutral. They are natural responses to our circumstances, designed to signal that something significant is happening in our internal or external environment. However, the intensity of our suffering often correlates with the emotion and how we react to it. Do we push it away, refusing to acknowledge its presence? Do we cling to it, allowing it to define our entire experience? Or do we observe, learn from, and let it pass in its own time?

Mindfulness and emotional intelligence are the keys to transforming our relationship with suffering. By becoming more aware of our emotions and understanding their transient nature, we can learn to experience them without becoming overwhelmed. This doesn't mean that the pain disappears, but rather that we develop a new capacity to coexist. We learn to recognize that emotions are like waves in the ocean – they rise, peak, and fall. Our suffering diminishes not when the waves stop coming but when we learn to swim.

Moreover, our emotions can be powerful guides, pointing us toward deeper truths about ourselves and our lives. They can reveal to us where we hold resistance, where we need to heal, and where we need to grow. By listening to our emotions with curiosity and compassion, we can uncover valuable insights that lead to personal transformation.

Our emotions and suffering are deeply intertwined, but they are not one and the same. By cultivating a mindful and compassionate relationship with our emotions, we can navigate suffering with greater ease and resilience. This journey is not about eliminating pain from our lives – that's an unrealistic goal. Instead, it's about learning to relate to our pain in a way that enriches our lives rather than diminishes them. Through this process, we discover that our greatest challenges can become our most profound teachers, leading us toward a deeper understanding of ourselves and a more fulfilling life.

Managing Emotional Pain

Emotional pain, much like physical pain, signals that something within us needs attention. It's a part of the human experience, yet we often need to work on managing it. The key to navigating this terrain lies in avoidance, understanding, and strategy.

First, let's acknowledge that emotions are complex. They can be overwhelming, mainly when they stem from deep-seated issues like loss, failure, or rejection. However, it's crucial to understand that these feelings are transient. They come and go, ebbing and flowing like the tide. Recognizing this can be liberating. It means that amid emotional turmoil, a part of you knows this pain is not permanent.

One practical approach to managing emotional pain is through mindfulness. This involves observing your emotions without judgment. Picture yourself sitting by a river, watching leaves (your emotions) float by. You're not trying to stop them, grab onto them, or question why they're there. You're simply noticing them. This practice can help create a space between you and your emotions, offering a sense of calm and detachment that makes the pain more manageable.

Another strategy is to express what you're feeling. This could be through talking to someone you trust, writing in a journal, or engaging in creative activities like painting or music. Expression provides an outlet for your emotions, preventing them from being bottled up inside. It's a way of honoring your feelings by giving them space and acknowledging their existence.

Physical activity is also a powerful tool. Exercise releases endorphins, chemicals in your brain that act as natural painkillers. Moreover, physical activity can help distract you from painful emotions, giving you a break from the cycle of negative thoughts that often accompany emotional pain.

Lastly, it's important to practice self-compassion. Be kind to yourself. Understand that it's okay not to be okay. You're doing the best you can with the tools you have. Self-compassion involves treating yourself with the same kindness, concern, and support you'd offer a good friend.

In conclusion, managing emotional pain is not about denying your feelings. It's about developing a toolkit that allows you to navigate through them. By practicing mindfulness, expressing your emotions, engaging in physical activity, and showing compassion, you're not just surviving; you're learning to thrive amidst the challenges. Remember, it's a journey. And like all journeys, it involves taking one step at a time.

The Power of Empathy

Empathy, often seen as the ability to understand and share the feelings of another, holds a transformative power in the realm of emotions and suffering. It's like a bridge connecting isolated islands, allowing us to reach out to others in their moments of pain and vulnerability. This connection, rooted in empathy, can significantly alter the course of healing, both for the giver and the receiver.

Picture navigation through the vast ocean, lost and alone. The direction is unclear, the waves high, and the sense of isolation overwhelming. Then, suddenly, you encounter another sailor. Though a stranger, this person understands the ocean currents, acknowledges your struggle, and chooses to navigate with you. The journey ahead remains the same, but the presence of a companion who empathizes with your situation changes everything. This is the essence of empathy in our lives. It doesn't erase our challenges, but sharing our emotional load makes the journey more bearable.

Empathy goes beyond mere sympathy, which is feeling

compassion for someone. It involves an emotional resonance, where we recognize the suffering of others and feel it to some extent. This shared emotional experience can lead to profound connections and support networks essential for navigating life's hardships.

Empathy can be a powerful tool for healing in the context of suffering. When someone empathizes with our pain, we feel seen, understood, and less alone. This validation is crucial because suffering often isolates us, making us feel as though we're trapped in a bubble of pain that no one else can see or understand. Empathy punctures that bubble, letting light in and showing us that our pain is recognized and shared.

Moreover, the act of expressing empathy has its own benefits. It fosters a sense of compassion and connection, reminding us of our shared humanity. In giving empathy, we also receive a gift—the realization that our own struggles have equipped us to be a source of comfort and understanding for others. This reciprocal nature of empathy enhances our emotional intelligence, enabling us to navigate our emotions and those of others with greater ease and understanding.

Empathy, therefore, is not just a passive feeling but an active force that can drive change, foster connections, and heal wounds. It challenges us to look beyond our own experiences, to step into the shoes of another, and to extend a hand in solidarity. Empathy shines as a beacon of hope in a world often marked by suffering, guiding us toward a more compassionate and connected existence.

Transforming Emotions

Emotions, those intricate threads woven into the fabric of our being, often dictate the tapestry of our lives in ways we scarcely understand. They can uplift or undo, connect or isolate. But what if we could transform these emotions, especially the ones that cause us suffering, into something empowering? This section delves into the heart of transforming emotions, guiding you through turning your emotional pain into a source of strength.

Imagine emotions as energy in motion. Like water, they can be turbulent or calm; with the proper techniques, we can learn to navigate through them rather than be overwhelmed. The first step in transforming emotions is acknowledging them. It's about giving yourself permission to feel, whether it's sadness, anger, or fear. These emotions are not your enemies but messengers, signaling areas within your life or your mindset that need attention.

Once acknowledged, the next step is understanding. Ask yourself, what is this emotion trying to tell me? Is there an underlying need or issue that still needs to be addressed? This step requires honesty and, sometimes, a bit of digging. It's only sometimes comfortable, but it's crucial. Understanding your emotions provides a roadmap to healing and growth.

Now, let's talk about the transformation. This doesn't mean erasing or suppressing your emotions. Instead, it's about channeling them towards something constructive. Anger can catalyze change, motivating you to address injustices or set boundaries. Sadness can deepen your empathy and connect you more profoundly with others. Fear can sharpen your focus and drive you to prepare thoroughly for challenges.

One effective method for transforming emotions is through mindfulness and meditation. These practices help you observe your emotions without judgment, allowing them to pass through you without taking hold. Another method is creative expression, whether it's through writing, painting, music, or any form of art that resonates with you. Creativity provides an outlet for your emotions, turning them into something tangible and, often, beautiful.

Lastly, it's essential to cultivate a support system. Sharing your feelings with trusted friends, family, or a therapist can provide new perspectives and remind you that you're not alone in your journey. Sometimes, verbalizing your emotions can lessen their intensity and help you see the path to transformation more clearly.

Transforming emotions is not a one-time event but a continuous process. It requires patience, practice, and perseverance. But the rewards are immense. By mastering this skill, you alleviate your suffering and open up new avenues for personal growth and fulfillment. Remember, the goal is not to become emotionless but to master your emotions, using them to build a more prosperous, more resilient life.

Chapter Summary

- Emotions are complex experiences that influence decisions, relationships, and well-being, indicating what is important or dangerous.
- Understanding emotions involves recognizing their role in shaping our perception of the world and guiding our responses to adversity, emphasizing the importance of a growth mindset.
- Emotions are transient and influenced by various factors, highlighting the importance of how we respond to them and the power of empathy in connecting with others.
- Emotional pain, like physical pain, signals a need for attention, advocating for mindfulness, expression, physical activity, and self-compassion as coping strategies.

- Emotional intelligence (EI) is crucial for recognizing, understanding, managing, and using emotions to navigate life's challenges. It emphasizes self-awareness, self-management, social awareness, and relationship management.
- Empathy, the ability to understand and share the feelings of others, plays a transformative role in healing and fostering connections, distinguishing itself from sympathy.
- Transforming emotions involves acknowledging, understanding, and channeling emotions constructively through mindfulness, creative expression, and cultivating a support system.
- The text underscores the continuous process of mastering emotions to alleviate suffering and promote personal growth. The goal is not to become emotionless but to use emotions as tools for a richer life.

4
COPING MECHANISMS

Healthy vs. Unhealthy Coping

When we talk about coping mechanisms, we're discussing the strategies and behaviors we employ to manage stress, adversity, and emotional pain. Coping mechanisms are crucial to our journey through life, especially when navigating the rough waters of suffering. However, not all coping mechanisms are created equal. There's a line—a sometimes blurry one—between healthy and unhealthy coping strategies. Understanding this distinction is vital for anyone looking to build resilience and foster a positive mindset in the face of life's inevitable challenges.

Healthy coping mechanisms are those strategies that contribute positively to our mental, emotional, and physical well-being. They're the tools that leave us feeling stronger, more empowered, and better equipped to face what comes next. These can range from seeking social support, engaging in physical activity, and practicing mindfulness to pursuing creative outlets. The common thread among these strategies is their ability to provide a constructive outlet for processing our emotions, leading to genuine healing and growth.

On the flip side, unhealthy coping mechanisms might provide a temporary escape or relief. Still, they often do so at a significant cost. These can include substance abuse, avoidance, denial, or self-harm. While they might seem to offer a quick fix, the relief is fleeting, and over time, they can compound the very problems we're trying to escape. Unhealthy coping mechanisms can trap us in a cycle of suffering, making it harder to address the root causes of our distress.

The key to distinguishing between healthy and unhealthy coping lies in self-awareness and honesty. It's about asking, "Does this behavior help me face my problems, or does it just push them away temporarily?" This question isn't always easy to answer, especially when we're in the thick of our struggles. Yet, it's crucial to developing resilience and a healthier mindset.

Adopting healthy coping mechanisms doesn't mean we won't feel pain or face hardship. Instead, it means we're choosing to face our suffering in a way that leads to healing and growth. It's about consciously navigating our struggles with strategies that build us up rather than tear us down.

As we explore coping mechanisms, remember that the journey towards healthier coping is a personal one. What works for one person might not work for another. The goal is to find the strategies that resonate with you, help you face your suffering head-on, and ultimately guide you toward a place of greater strength and peace.

Building Resilience

Resilience stands as a beacon of hope in life's journey, guiding us through suffering and adversity. It's not just about bouncing back; it's about growing, learning, and becoming stronger in the face of challenges. Building resilience is akin to constructing a house. It requires a solid foundation, the right materials, and a good plan. Let's explore how we can lay down the foundation and gather the materials to fortify our resilience.

First, understand that resilience is not innate to a lucky few. It's a skill, a muscle everyone can develop and strengthen over time. It begins with the mindset. A growth mindset, the belief that we can improve and adapt through effort and learning, is the cornerstone of resilience. It empowers us to view challenges not as insurmountable obstacles but as opportunities for growth.

Next, let's talk about the needed materials: self-awareness, emotional intelligence, and a support network. Self-awareness allows us to recognize our emotions, understand our reactions, and identify our strengths and weaknesses. Emotional intelligence builds on this, enabling us to manage our emotions and empathize with others, fostering connections that can strengthen us in tough times. And a support network? The scaffolding holds us up when we struggle to stand independently.

Now, for the plan. Building resilience requires a proactive approach. Start by setting small, achievable goals. These are the bricks that will build your resilience house. Each goal achieved is a victory, no matter how small, reinforcing your belief in overcoming challenges. Embrace challenges as they come, viewing them as chances to practice resilience. And when you stumble, remember, it's not about never falling; it's about learning how to get back up.

Finally, practice self-care and mindfulness. These finishing touches turn the house of resilience into a home. Self-care ensures you're physically, emotionally, and mentally prepared to face life's challenges. Mindfulness keeps you anchored in the present, helping you navigate through storms with a clear mind and a calm heart.

Building resilience is a journey, not a destination. It's a process of continuous learning and adaptation. Like any skill, it requires practice, patience, and perseverance. But the rewards are immeasurable. With resilience, you're not just surviving; you're thriving, ready to face whatever life throws your way with strength, grace, and a smile.

Mindfulness and Meditation

We find ourselves at the heart of our exploration of coping mechanisms at the doorstep of mindfulness and meditation. These practices, often intertwined, serve as powerful tools for mental and emotional well-being. I've briefly mentioned mindfulness and meditation here and here. Still, it's time to dive into how they can be pivotal in managing suffering and fostering a resilient mindset.

Mindfulness, in its essence, is the practice of being fully present and engaged in the moment without judgment. It's about noticing the details of your surroundings, the sensations in your body, and the thoughts passing through your mind. Imagine you're walking through a garden. Instead of being lost in thought about what you need to do later, you're acutely aware of the colors of the flowers, the sound of the leaves rustling in the wind, and the feeling of the sun on your skin. This heightened awareness can be a sanctuary from the relentless pace of modern life and its associated stresses.

Meditation, however, often involves setting aside time to sit quietly and focus your mind. This can be on your breath, a mantra, or even the sensations in your body. The goal isn't to empty your mind or achieve some state of enlightenment overnight. Instead, it's about training your mind to return to your focus point whenever you notice it wandering. It's normal for thoughts to drift in, but the practice lies in gently bringing your attention back, time and again.

So, how do these practices help with suffering? First, they teach us to observe our thoughts and feelings without getting swept away by them. It's like learning to sit on the bank of a river, watching your thoughts flow by rather than being caught in the current. This detachment allows us to recognize that while we may not have control over everything that happens to us, we have a choice in how we respond.

Moreover, mindfulness and meditation can lower stress, reduce symptoms of anxiety and depression, and improve sleep. These benefits, in turn, can make us more resilient in the face of life's challenges. They remind us that suffering is part of the human condition, but it doesn't have to define our existence.

Incorporating mindfulness and meditation into your life doesn't require hours of your day or a mountain retreat (though that sounds lovely). It can be as simple as taking a few deep breaths before starting your car, enjoying your morning coffee without the distraction of your phone, or dedicating five minutes to meditation each day. The key is consistency and patience with yourself.

As we navigate the complexities of suffering and seek

ways to cope, mindfulness and meditation stand out as beacons of hope. They offer a path to endure life's storms and find peace amidst them. So, I invite you to explore these practices. Start small, stay curious, and be gentle with yourself. The journey toward a more mindful and resilient life is worth the effort.

The Role of Community

In the labyrinth of life, where suffering and mindset intertwine, the role of community emerges as a beacon of hope and a source of strength. It's fascinating how the collective spirit of a community can act as a powerful coping mechanism, offering solace and support in times of distress. Let's delve into this concept, shall we?

Imagine, for a moment, you're navigating a particularly rough patch in life. The kind that feels like a relentless storm, leaving you yearning for a sliver of sunlight. In these moments, the community around you can become your shelter. Whether it's family, friends, or even a group of strangers bound by similar experiences, the sense of belonging and understanding they provide can be incredibly healing.

Communities are built on the foundation of shared experiences and mutual support. They offer a unique space where individuals can openly share their struggles without the fear of judgment. This act of sharing not only lightens the individual burden but also fosters a sense of solidarity. It's a powerful reminder that you're not alone in your journey and that others have weathered similar storms.

Moreover, communities often serve as a reservoir of collective wisdom. They are a source of invaluable advice, coping strategies, and resources that can aid in navigating the complexities of suffering. From practical support, like helping with day-to-day tasks during tough times, to emotional support, like offering a listening ear or a shoulder to cry on, the community's role is multifaceted.

But a community's most profound impact lies in its ability to inspire hope. Witnessing others overcome their adversities or knowing some people care can reignite the flame of hope within us. This hope often catalyzes a shift in mindset from despair to resilience and growth.

It's important, however, to recognize that a community's strength lies not just in receiving support but also in giving it. Supporting others can be incredibly therapeutic and empowering. It reinforces our sense of purpose and connection, further solidifying the community's role as a vital coping mechanism.

In conclusion, the role of the community in coping with suffering and fostering a resilient mindset cannot be overstated. It represents the power of collective empathy, support, and hope. As we navigate the ups and downs of life, let us remember to lean on our communities and to be a pillar of support for others. For it is together, as a united front, that we can weather the storms and emerge stronger.

Finding Meaning in Suffering

In life, suffering often appears as dark threads contrasting sharply against the brighter hues of joy and contentment. Yet, these very threads add depth and complexity to the overall picture, offering a richness that would otherwise be absent. This notion of finding meaning in suffering isn't just philosophical musing; it's a vital coping mechanism that can transform our experience of pain into something profoundly transformative.

Let's consider the concept of resilience for a moment. It's easy to admire resilience in others, but recognizing it in ourselves during suffering can be challenging. Yet, precisely in these moments, we can forge resilience as steel tempered by fire. This process isn't about denying the pain or hardship but seeking a deeper understanding of its role in our lives.

I remember when I faced a personal crisis that shook the foundations of my world. It was a period marked by sleepless nights and a heart so heavy it felt like it could break at any moment. Amid this turmoil, I stumbled upon a quote.

> "In the depth of winter, I finally learned that within me there lay an invincible summer."
>
> — ALBERT CAMUS

This simple sentence, penned by Camus, became a beacon of hope. It didn't erase the pain, but it helped me to see it in a different light. I began to understand that this suffering was not just a period of loss and despair but also a profound opportunity for growth and self-discovery.

Finding meaning in suffering is not a one-size-fits-all solution. For some, it may come through the pursuit of creative expression, channeling their pain into art, music, or writing. For others, it might be found in the service of others, discovering a sense of purpose in helping those who are also struggling. And for many, it's in the quiet reflection, a turning inward to explore the lessons hidden within the heartache.

The journey through suffering is deeply personal, and the meaning we derive from it is unique to each of us. However, the common thread that binds these experiences is the potential for transformation. By embracing our suffering as a part of our story, not as the entirety of it, we open ourselves to the possibility of emerging from the depths not just unscathed but enriched.

As we navigate the complexities of suffering, let us remember that it's not merely an obstacle to be overcome but a path to deeper understanding and resilience. In the words of Frankl, a psychiatrist and Holocaust survivor:

> "When we are no longer able to change a situation, we are challenged to change ourselves."
>
> — VIKTOR FRANKL

In this change, this search for meaning amidst the suffering, we find the strength to continue, grow, and ultimately thrive.

Self-Care Strategies

Self-care emerges as a strategy and a vital component of resilience and healing in coping with suffering. It's a concept that's both simple and profound, often overlooked in the hustle of daily life. Yet, it holds the key to surviving and thriving amidst life's inevitable challenges.

Self-care is the intentional act of taking time to care for oneself holistically—physically, emotionally, mentally, and spiritually. It's about recognizing when your resources are running low and knowing how to replenish them. This isn't about indulgence or selfishness; it's about respect for oneself and the understanding that you can't pour from an empty cup.

Physically, self-care can be as basic as ensuring you're

getting enough sleep, eating nutritious foods, and engaging in regular physical activity. These actions lay the foundation for a strong body capable of withstanding stress and recovering from illness. It's remarkable how much a balanced diet and a little exercise can do for your mood and mindset.

Emotionally and mentally, self-care might involve setting boundaries to protect your energy, seeking therapy or counseling when needed, and engaging in activities that bring joy and relaxation. It's also about cultivating a positive inner dialogue, challenging negative thoughts, and practicing gratitude. Remember, it's okay to ask for help. Seeking support is a sign of strength, not weakness.

Spiritually, self-care can mean different things to different people. For some, it involves meditation, prayer, or connecting with nature. For others, it's about finding purpose and meaning in life, perhaps through volunteering or creative pursuits. Whatever it looks like for you, spiritual self-care is about connecting with something greater than yourself and finding peace within.

Incorporating self-care into your daily routine doesn't have to be overwhelming. Start small. Choose one or two practices to focus on and gradually build from there. The key is consistency. Even on your busiest days, try to carve out a few minutes for yourself. These small, daily acts of self-care accumulate over time, leading to profound changes in how you cope with suffering and adversity.

Remember, the journey through suffering is not merely about enduring but learning, growing, and emerging stronger on the other side. Self-care is not just a strategy for coping; it's a way of living—a commitment to honoring and nurturing the one body, mind, and soul you've been given.

Chapter Summary

- Coping mechanisms are strategies to manage stress, adversity, and emotional pain, with a distinction between healthy and unhealthy approaches.
- Healthy coping mechanisms, such as seeking social support, engaging in physical activity, and practicing mindfulness, positively impact mental, emotional, and physical well-being.
- Unhealthy coping mechanisms, like substance abuse and avoidance, offer temporary relief but can worsen problems over time, trapping individuals in a cycle of suffering.
- Distinguishing between healthy and unhealthy coping requires self-awareness and honesty. One must ask whether a behavior truly addresses problems or merely postpones them.

- Building resilience involves developing a growth mindset, self-awareness, emotional intelligence, and a support network, along with setting achievable goals and practicing self-care.
- Mindfulness and meditation are key practices in managing suffering and building resilience, focusing on being present and engaged without judgment.
- The community plays a crucial role in coping by providing a sense of belonging, shared experiences, mutual support, and hope, emphasizing the importance of giving and receiving support.
- Finding meaning in suffering and practicing self-care is vital for transforming pain into growth and ensuring holistic well-being, emphasizing the importance of small, consistent acts of self-care.

5

THE POWER OF RELATIONSHIPS

Social Support Systems

In life, where suffering and mindset intertwine, the power of relationships emerges as a beacon of hope and resilience. At the heart of these relationships lies the foundation of social support systems, an intricate web of connections that holds the potential to uplift, heal, and transform.

Imagine, for a moment, you're navigating a stormy sea. The waves are relentless, the sky is a blanket of grey, and the shore seems like a distant dream. This is the journey of suffering—a path familiar to many yet uniquely experienced by all. Now, picture a lighthouse on the horizon, its light piercing through the fog, guiding you to safety. This lighthouse represents your social support system, pivotal in overcoming suffering and fostering a resilient mindset.

Social support systems are not a one-size-fits-all solution. They are as diverse as the individuals they serve, encompassing family, friends, community groups, and professional networks. These systems provide emotional comfort, practical assistance, and a sense of belonging—three crucial pillars in the face of adversity.

Emotional comfort comes in the form of empathy, understanding, and the simple yet profound act of listening. It's the shoulder to lean on when the world's weight feels unbearable. On the other hand, practical assistance includes tangible help like running errands for someone ill or offering financial support during tough times. Lastly, shared experiences and the mutual exchange of care and compassion foster a sense of belonging. Together, these pillars construct a safety net, cushioning the fall when life's challenges threaten to overwhelm.

The significance of social support systems extends beyond the immediate relief they provide. Research has consistently shown that individuals with strong social connections tend to have better mental health, higher levels of self-esteem, and a more optimistic outlook on life. In essence, these systems do not just help us survive; they help us thrive.

However, building and maintaining a robust social support system has its challenges. It requires effort, vulnerability, and a willingness to give and receive help. It's about nurturing relationships, being present, and showing up—not just in times of crisis but also in quiet moments. It's a reciprocal dance of support that, over time, weaves a tapestry of interconnected lives.

Social support systems play a transformative role in the context of mindset and suffering. They remind us that we are not alone in our struggles, that our feelings are valid, and that hope is never out of reach. They encourage us to shift our perspective, see beyond the immediate pain, and embrace the possibility of growth and healing.

As we journey through the chapters of this book, exploring the intricate relationship between mindset and suffering, let us not underestimate the power of relationships. Let us recognize and cherish our social support systems, for they are the lighthouses guiding us through the storm, leading us toward a horizon where resilience, hope, and healing await.

The Impact of Loneliness

Loneliness, often misunderstood, is a complex emotion that can significantly impact our mental and physical health. It's not just about being alone; it's about feeling disconnected, unseen, and unsupported. Loneliness acts as a silent predator in relationships, creeping into our lives when connections with others are superficial, strained, or absent.

The effects of loneliness can be profound. Research has shown that it can increase the risk of depression, anxiety, and other mental health issues. But it doesn't stop there. Loneliness has been linked to physical health problems as well, such as heart disease and a weakened immune system. It's as if our bodies tell us that social connections are not just a luxury but a necessity.

But here's the kicker: loneliness can also be a powerful motivator for change. It can push us to look closer at our relationships and encourage us to foster more profound, meaningful connections. When we acknowledge our loneliness, we begin the journey towards healing, not just by seeking out others but also by turning inward and addressing our own role in our isolation.

Building meaningful relationships requires effort and vulnerability. It's about more than just spending time with people; it's about being present, listening deeply, and showing up for others in a way that lets them know they truly matter. It's about creating a space where everyone feels seen and heard.

The power of relationships in combating loneliness cannot be overstated. A robust support system buffers against life's challenges, providing a sense of belonging and security. These connections remind us that we're not alone in our struggles and that there's a community of people who care about us and are willing to stand by us through thick and thin.

So, if you're feeling lonely, know it's a signal, not a sentence. It's an invitation to connect and rediscover the joy of being part of something bigger than yourself. Remember, the quality of our relationships, not the quantity, truly matters. In the end, these connections have the power to heal us, transform our suffering into strength, and remind us of the beauty of being human.

Building Meaningful Connections

In the heart of our journey through understanding mindset and suffering, we've navigated the terrains of personal pain, the resilience of the human spirit, and the transformative power of emotions. Now, as we delve into the essence of building meaningful connections, we find ourselves at a crucial juncture that underscores the profound impact relationships have on our ability to thrive amidst adversity.

Imagine navigating through a dense fog, the mist so thick it swallows the light, making the path ahead uncertain. This fog is akin to the suffering many of us face at various times. Now, imagine finding a break in the fog where the light breaks through; there, you find others navigating their dense fogs. This is the power of meaningful connections. They become the breaks in our lives, spaces where light breaks through, offering warmth, guidance, and companionship.

Building meaningful connections isn't about accumulating a vast network of acquaintances but about fostering deep, genuine relationships with people who understand, support, and challenge us. These connections offer a mirror to our own selves, reflecting back to us who we are and who we can become. They provide a safe space to share our vulnerabilities, celebrate our strengths, and, most importantly, remind us that we are not alone in our struggles.

Building these connections often begins with a simple yet profound act of reaching out. It's about taking the first step to engage with someone on a level beyond the superficial. This could be as simple as sharing a personal story, expressing genuine interest in another's experiences, or offering support without expectation of reciprocity. In these moments of authentic exchange, the seeds of meaningful connections are sown.

However, it's essential to recognize that not all relationships will evolve into meaningful connections, and that's okay. The key is to remain open, patient, and discerning. It's about quality, not quantity. A few deep and meaningful relationships can be far more supportive and enriching than numerous superficial ones.

Moreover, in the context of suffering, these connections become lifelines. They remind us of our resilience, offer new perspectives, and provide comfort during our darkest times. They can also be powerful catalysts for healing, helping us navigate our way out of suffering and into the light of understanding and acceptance.

Building meaningful connections is about cultivating a garden of relationships where empathy, support, and genuine care can flourish. It's about recognizing that our journey through suffering is not a solitary trek but a shared voyage. And it's in the company of those we connect with deeply that we find the strength to continue, the courage to heal, and the joy in living fully despite the inevitable challenges life throws our way.

So, as we move forward, let's commit to reaching out, building bridges of understanding, and nurturing the connections that illuminate our paths. For, in the end, it's through these meaningful connections that we discover the most powerful antidote to suffering: the enduring strength of human connection and the unassailable hope it brings.

Relationships and Healing

In the healing realm, relationships' significance cannot be overstated. This theme resonates deeply, not just in the abstract but in the very fabric of our daily lives. The power of a meaningful connection can often serve as the bridge between suffering and recovery. This concept is both simple and profound.

Consider, for a moment, how a single conversation can alter a day. A kind word from a friend, a compassionate look, or even a shared silence can carry the weight of therapy in distress. In these interactions, we find our burdens lightened, and our spirits lifted, not by grand gestures but by the simple act of being understood and accepted.

This isn't just theoretical. I recall a period when the shadows seemed particularly long, and hope felt like a concept designed for others, not for me. During this time, a friend, let's name him John for confidentiality's sake, reached out, not with answers, but with presence. We shared stories, often not directly related to my suffering, and in those stories, I found pieces of myself I thought were lost. This connection didn't erase my challenges but provided a lifeline, a reminder that I wasn't navigating my troubles alone. It was a subtle yet powerful testament to the healing potential of relationships.

The science backs this up, too. Research has consistently shown that social support can significantly impact our mental and physical health. It can lower anxiety, decrease depression, and even improve our immune system. But beyond the numbers and the studies lies a truth that most of us understand instinctively: we are social beings, and our connections with others form the cornerstone of our well-being.

In the context of suffering, relationships act as a mirror, reflecting back to us our pain and our capacity for resilience and joy. They remind us of our strengths, help us to navigate our vulnerabilities, and encourage us to see beyond our current circumstances. This is not to say that relationships can or should replace professional help when needed. Instead, they complement the healing journey, adding layers of support and understanding unique to the bonds we share with those around us.

As we delve deeper into the power of relationships, it's essential to recognize that the quality of these connections matters more than the quantity. A few deep, meaningful relationships can offer more support than a vast network of superficial ones. It's about finding those people who can sit with us in our moments of darkness and celebrate with us in our times of joy without judgment or expectation.

Ultimately, the healing journey is as much about reconnecting with ourselves as it is about connecting with others. Through the lens of our relationships, we learn not just to endure suffering but to grow from it, to find meaning in it, and ultimately, to move beyond it. This is the power of relationships in the healing process—a power that is both profoundly human and deeply transformative.

Navigating Conflict

Conflict is as inevitable in relationships as the setting sun. Yet, it's not the presence of conflict that defines a relationship's strength but rather how it's navigated. Like steering a ship through stormy seas, the art of navigating conflict requires skill, patience, and a deep understanding of the other's perspective.

Let's consider a personal anecdote to illustrate this point. A few years ago, I was embroiled in a disagreement with a close friend. The issue at hand was trivial, yet our emotions were anything but. As voices raised and tempers flared, it became clear that the path we were on would lead to nothing but mutual resentment. It was a pivotal moment that required a choice: to continue down the path of conflict or to seek a resolution. Choosing the latter, we took a step back, allowing ourselves the space to cool down. When we reconvened, it was to listen, truly listen, to each other's perspectives. This simple act of empathy transformed our conflict into a bridge, strengthening our bond in ways we hadn't anticipated.

This anecdote underscores a fundamental truth about conflict: it's not the enemy of relationships but an opportunity for growth. The key lies in our approach. When faced with conflict, the first step is recognizing the emotions at play. Acknowledge your feelings, but don't let them steer the ship. Instead, approach the situation with a mindset geared towards resolution. This involves active listening, a term that goes beyond merely hearing words. It's about understanding the emotions and intentions behind those words. Doing so creates a space where both parties feel heard and valued.

Another crucial aspect of navigating conflict is the willingness to compromise. This doesn't mean sacrificing your values but finding a middle ground where both parties can agree. It's about flexibility and the understanding that sometimes, the relationship is more important than being right.

Finally, it's essential to learn from the conflict. Each disagreement offers valuable insights into the dynamics of your relationship. By reflecting on what triggered the conflict and how it was resolved, you can identify patterns and areas for improvement. This reflective practice not only helps prevent similar conflicts in the future but also deepens your understanding and appreciation of each other.

In conclusion, navigating conflict within relationships is a delicate dance. It requires empathy, active listening, compromise, and reflection. By embracing these principles, we can transform conflict from a source of suffering into a catalyst for growth and deeper connection. Remember, the goal is not to avoid conflict but to learn how to navigate it with grace and understanding.

JAMES CONANT

The Role of Love and Compassion

In the heart of every human being lies an innate desire for connection, a yearning that transcends the superficial layers of our existence and touches the very core of who we are. This longing for connection, for a bond that goes beyond the mere exchange of words, is where the role of love and compassion becomes undeniably powerful. We find the most profound healing in the gentle touch of a mother, the reassuring hug of a friend, and the silent empathy of a stranger.

Love and compassion are not just emotions; they are forces of nature capable of transforming suffering into a shared experience that unites us in our humanity. They remind us that we are not alone in our struggles and that others understand and feel our pain. This shared understanding builds the bridges that connect our isolated islands of suffering, creating a network of support that can withstand the storms of life.

But why are love and compassion crucial in our relationships, especially when dealing with suffering? The answer lies in their ability to soften the edges of our pain, to bring light into the darkest corners of our existence. When we act with compassion, we acknowledge the suffering of another as if it were our own, offering a kind of solace that words often fail to convey. Love, in its purest form, acts as a balm, soothing the wounds that life inflicts upon us.

The power of these forces is not just in their ability to heal but in their capacity to inspire change. Love and compassion can motivate us to look beyond our own suffering to reach out and help others in their moments of need. They encourage us to build communities based on shared interests, mutual care, and understanding. In these communities, we learn that our suffering, no matter how personal it may seem, is part of a larger human experience. Through this realization, we find not just healing but a sense of purpose and belonging.

However, cultivating love and compassion in our relationships requires effort and intentionality. It demands that we look beyond our prejudices and biases and listen with open hearts and minds. It asks us to be vulnerable, share our own suffering, and be present in the suffering of others. This can be challenging, uncomfortable, and even painful at times. But it is in this space of shared vulnerability that a genuine connection is forged.

As we navigate the complexities of human relationships, let us remember the transformative power of love and compassion. Let us strive to be light sources for each other, offering support and understanding in times of darkness. For it is through our connections with others that we find the strength to overcome suffering, to grow, and to thrive. Love and compassion are not just antidotes to suffering; they are the very essence of what it means to be human.

Chapter Summary

- Social support systems are crucial for overcoming suffering and fostering resilience, providing emotional comfort, practical assistance, and a sense of belonging.
- Strong social connections lead to better mental health, self-esteem, and optimism, but building and maintaining these connections requires effort and vulnerability.
- Loneliness, characterized by feeling disconnected and unsupported, can lead to mental and physical health issues but also motivates the pursuit of meaningful relationships.
- Meaningful connections, deep and genuine, offer support, challenge us, and remind us we're not alone, playing a pivotal role in navigating personal suffering.
- Relationships significantly impact healing, acting as a bridge between suffering and recovery through simple acts of understanding and acceptance.

- Navigating conflict within relationships involves empathy, active listening, compromise, and learning from disagreements to foster growth and deeper connections.
- Love and compassion in relationships transform suffering into shared experiences, uniting us in our humanity and inspiring communities based on mutual care.
- Cultivating love and compassion demands looking beyond prejudices, vulnerability, and presence in others' suffering, which is essential for proper connection and overcoming challenges.

6

OVERCOMING OBSTACLES

Identifying Obstacles

The first step in overcoming obstacles is to identify them. It sounds straightforward. But here's the catch: often, the most significant barriers to our progress are not the external challenges we face but the internal ones. Yes, I'm talking about our mindset, fears, and preconceived notions about suffering.

Let's start with mindsct. As we've learned, it's a powerful tool and a formidable obstacle. To recap the previous sections, a fixed mindset convinces us that our abilities, intelligence, and emotional capacity are static. This belief limits our growth and makes us more susceptible to suffering because we see challenges as threats rather than growth opportunities. On the other hand, a growth mindset encourages us to embrace challenges, learn from them, and ultimately overcome them.

Fear is another significant obstacle. It's natural to fear the unknown or fear failure. Still, when fear paralyzes us, it prevents us from taking the necessary steps to move forward. It's like being stuck at the starting line, watching opportunities pass because we're too afraid to take the first step.

Preconceived notions about suffering also play a role. Many of us have been conditioned to view suffering as purely negative, something to be avoided at all costs. However, this perspective can limit our understanding and appreciation of the depth of human experience. Suffering, while undoubtedly challenging, can also catalyze growth, self-discovery, and transformation.

Identifying these obstacles is not about blaming ourselves or dwelling on our shortcomings. Instead, it's about gaining clarity. It's about understanding the internal barriers that hold us back so we can begin dismantling them. This process is challenging and quick, but it is necessary. By recognizing the obstacles within us, we empower ourselves to overcome them and move closer to a life of less suffering and more fulfillment.

So, as we move forward, let's keep this in mind: the journey of overcoming obstacles is as much about looking inward as it is about facing the challenges. With this understanding, we're equipped to tackle the obstacles we already know and prepare ourselves to face the ones we have yet to discover.

The Role of Perseverance

In the heart of every challenge lies an opportunity for growth, a sentiment echoed through the ages yet often forgotten in the heat of our struggles. Perseverance, the steadfast persistence in doing something despite difficulty or delay in achieving success, is a virtue and a necessity in overcoming obstacles. It is the fuel that powers us through the darkest nights and the roughest storms.

Let me share a story about my friend; let's call her Mary for confidentiality's sake. Mary found herself facing what seemed like an insurmountable obstacle during a time when everything that could go wrong did. It felt like life was testing her resolve, pushing her to her limits. The details are mundane, as most personal battles involve a series of professional setbacks and personal losses. Yet, Mary learned the most valuable lesson about perseverance in this crucible of suffering.

She discovered perseverance is not about the absence of doubt or fear but moving forward despite it. It's about holding on to hope when despair seems easier. It's about taking one more step when your body screams to stop. This realization didn't come in a moment of triumph but in the quiet determination to try just once more, to give it one more day.

This journey taught Mary that perseverance is not a solitary endeavor. It's nurtured by the support we give and receive, the stories of resilience we share, and the understanding that our struggles, while unique, are also universal. It's a collective strength woven through the fabric of human experience that reminds us we are not alone.

In the context of mindset and suffering, perseverance bridges enduring hardship and emerging stronger. It's the process through which a fixed mindset that sees obstacles as insurmountable barriers can transform into a growth mindset, which views challenges as opportunities to learn and grow. This shift doesn't happen overnight. It requires patience, effort, and, most importantly, perseverance.

The role of perseverance in overcoming obstacles cannot be overstated. It's the quiet voice at the end of the day whispering, "try again tomorrow." It's the resilience to face life's challenges head-on and the wisdom to know that suffering, while a part of life, doesn't define us. Our actions, our persistence, and our ability to persevere do.

So, as we navigate the complexities of mindset and suffering, let's remember the power of perseverance. It's a testament to our strength, a beacon of hope in times of despair, and a reminder that no matter the obstacle, we have the power to overcome within us.

Learning from Failure

Failure is a strict teacher, but it's also one of the most effective. It's not just about the setbacks; it's about what we learn from them and how we move forward. This section is dedicated to understanding the value hidden within our failures and how to harness them to overcome obstacles.

Let's start with a simple truth: everyone fails. It's a universal experience, as common as breathing. Yet, society often paints failure negatively as something to be avoided at all costs. This perception couldn't be further from the truth. Failure is not the opposite of success; it's a stepping stone towards it.

Think of failure as feedback—information. When something doesn't work out, it tells you that a change in approach is needed. This is where the growth mindset kicks in. Instead of seeing failure as a reflection of your abilities, view it as an opportunity to grow, improve, and innovate. This shift in perspective is crucial. It transforms the emotional landscape of failure from one of despair to one of opportunity.

Learning from failure requires introspection. Ask yourself, "What went wrong?" and "What can I do differently next time?" These questions are simple yet powerful. They encourage you to look beyond the immediate pain of failure and focus on the lessons it offers. This process of reflection and adaptation is at the heart of resilience. It builds mental and emotional muscles like physical exercise builds physical strength.

Moreover, sharing your failures and the lessons learned can be incredibly empowering, not just for you but also for others. It created a sense of community and shared humanity. Knowing that others have faced similar challenges and have come out stronger on the other side provides hope and encouragement.

However, it's important to note that learning from failure doesn't mean you won't experience disappointment or frustration. These feelings are natural. The key is not to dwell on them. Acknowledge your emotions, give yourself time to process, and shift your focus to learning and moving forward.

In essence, failure is not the end of the road; it's just a bend. It's an integral part of the journey towards success. By embracing failure, learning from it, and using it as fuel for growth, you equip yourself with the resilience and perseverance needed to overcome obstacles and achieve your goals. Remember, the most successful people are not those who never fail but those who never give up.

Adaptability and Change

Adaptability and change emerge as pivotal allies in overcoming obstacles. It's about embracing the fluidity of life and understanding that the only constant is change itself. This realization doesn't come easy. It's a truth that often dawns on us not in moments of tranquility but amidst the storms of challenge and adversity.

I remember a time when I was faced with a sudden, unexpected change in my career path. It felt as though the rug had been pulled from under my feet. The future I had envisioned seemed to crumble before my eyes. Yet, in this moment of uncertainty, I discovered adaptability's true essence. Instead of resisting the change, I learned to lean into it, to see it not as the end of the road but as a detour leading to new horizons. This personal experience taught me that adaptability isn't just about surviving; it's about thriving. It's about finding ways to flourish even when the external circumstances are less than favorable.

Adaptability and change require a mindset that views obstacles not as insurmountable barriers but as opportunities for growth and learning. It's about developing resilience that allows us to bounce back from setbacks, armed with new knowledge and a deeper understanding of our strengths and capabilities.

To cultivate this adaptability, we must first acknowledge our resistance to change. It's a natural human tendency to seek comfort and stability. However, growth often lies just beyond the boundaries of our comfort zones. By challenging ourselves to step into the unknown, we expand our capacity for adaptability.

Moreover, adaptability involves a proactive approach

to problem-solving. It's about anticipating potential challenges and preparing ourselves mentally and emotionally to face them. This doesn't mean living in a state of constant anxiety over what might go wrong. Instead, it's about equipping ourselves with the tools and strategies needed to navigate the unpredictable waters of life.

Finally, adaptability is about maintaining a positive outlook in adversity. It's about trusting in our ability to adapt and find new paths forward, even when the destination is unclear. This positive outlook acts as a beacon of hope, guiding us through the darkest times and reminding us that every obstacle presents an opportunity for growth.

In essence, adaptability and change are not just strategies for overcoming obstacles; they are essential life skills that enable us to navigate the complexities of the human experience. By embracing change and learning to adapt, we open ourselves up to a world of possibilities. We learn that every obstacle, no matter how daunting, carries the seeds of opportunity and transformation within it.

Setting and Achieving Goals

In overcoming obstacles, setting and achieving goals is a beacon of hope and a testament to human resilience. It's not just about the end result but the transformation within us as we navigate the challenges. This transformation is deeply personal and unique to each individual's journey.

Setting and achieving goals is akin to navigating a complex maze. There will be dead ends and detours, but with perseverance and adaptability, the path becomes clearer. It requires a balance of ambition and realism, of dreaming big while grounding those dreams in actionable steps. This balance is crucial, as it keeps us anchored to our purpose while allowing us to reach for the stars.

Moreover, setting and achieving goals is not a solitary journey. It's enriched by the support and encouragement of those around us. Sharing our goals with trusted friends or mentors can give us a sense of accountability and a support network. This communal aspect of goal setting is often overlooked but is integral to our success.

Setting and achieving goals is a dynamic and transformative process. It's about more than just ticking off items on a list; it's about the growth, learning, and resilience we develop along the way. As we navigate the obstacles, let us remember that each step forward, no matter how small, is a victory in its own right. Ultimately, these small victories pave the way for us to overcome the larger obstacles that life throws us.

The Power of Persistence

In the heart of every challenge lies an opportunity for growth. This is the essence of persistence. It's not just about stubbornly pushing forward; it's about embracing the journey, learning from each setback, and finding the strength to continue. Persistence is the silent force that turns obstacles into stepping stones, transforming what seems impossible today into tomorrow's victories.

Let me share a little story. Once, I decided to run a marathon. Now, I'm no athlete. My idea of exercise was a leisurely stroll to the fridge. But there I was, lacing up my running shoes, determined. The training was brutal. My muscles screamed, my lungs gasped, and every fiber of my being questioned my sanity. There were days when giving up seemed like the only rational choice. Yet, in those moments of doubt and pain, I discovered the true power of persistence. Each step became a testament to my resolve in running and every aspect of life. Crossing that finish line wasn't just about completing a race; it was a profound lesson in the strength of the human spirit when fueled by persistence.

This story, while personal, isn't unique. It mirrors the journey many of us face when confronted with obstacles. The path to overcoming challenges is more complex. It's fraught with setbacks, detours, and moments of uncertainty. Yet, persistence guides us through the darkness, offering a glimmer of hope when all seems lost.

Persistence is not an innate trait bestowed upon a lucky few. It's a skill honed through practice and determination. It begins with setting small, achievable goals and celebrating each victory, no matter how minor. It's about understanding that failure isn't the opposite of success; it's a vital part of the journey. Each setback offers invaluable lessons, providing insights that pave the way for future triumphs.

Moreover, persistence is fueled by passion. When deeply committed to our goals, finding the strength to persevere becomes second nature. It's this passion that ignites our resolve, transforming dreams into reality. But persistence also requires flexibility. Sometimes, the path we've charted could be more viable. Being persistent doesn't mean being rigid. It's about adapting, learning, and finding new ways to overcome the hurdles that stand in our way.

In essence, the power of persistence lies in its ability to transform. It molds us into resilient beings, capable of withstanding the trials and tribulations life throws our way. It teaches us that within us lies an indomitable spirit, ready to rise in adversity. So, as we journey through the chapters of our lives, let us embrace persistence as our guide, knowing that it's not just about reaching the destination but about growing stronger with every step we take.

Chapter Summary

- Identifying obstacles is crucial in overcoming them, with mindset, fear, and preconceived notions about suffering being significant internal barriers.
- A fixed mindset sees abilities as static and limits growth, while a growth mindset views challenges as opportunities for growth.
- Fear can paralyze progress, preventing individuals from taking necessary steps forward.
- Suffering, though challenging, can serve as a catalyst for growth, self-discovery, and transformation.
- Perseverance, or persistence in the face of difficulty, is essential for overcoming obstacles and is fueled by support, resilience stories, and a shift from a fixed to a growth mindset.
- Failure should be viewed as feedback and an opportunity for growth, requiring introspection and a shift in perspective to learn from setbacks.
- Adaptability and embracing change are pivotal in overcoming obstacles, involving a proactive

approach to problem-solving, and maintaining a positive outlook.

- Setting and achieving goals involves breaking down larger objectives into manageable steps, celebrating small victories, and being supported by a network of encouragement from others.

7
THE SEARCH FOR MEANING

What is Meaning?

At the heart of our journey through life, amidst the highs and lows, the joy and suffering, lies a fundamental question that has puzzled philosophers, theologians, and everyday seekers alike: What is meaning? This question, simple in its structure, is profound in its depth, touching the very core of our existence.

Meaning, in its broadest sense, is the significance we attach to our lives, the value we find in our experiences, and the purpose we see in our actions. It's what fuels our mornings, what we ponder during sleepless nights, and what we seek in the pages of books, the words of mentors, and the quiet of our own reflections. But meaning is not a one-size-fits-all answer tucked away in some ancient text or hidden in the advice of the wise. It's deeply personal, ever-evolving, and as unique as our fingerprints.

Consider for a moment the diversity of human pursuits. For some, meaning is found in pursuing knowledge, understanding the universe's mysteries, or unraveling the complexities of the human mind. For others, it's in creating art, expressing the inexpressible through paint, music, or words. Then, some find meaning in the service of others, dedicating their lives to alleviating suffering, fighting for justice, or caring for the vulnerable. And yet, for some, meaning is in the simplicity of life itself – the warmth of the sun on their face, the laughter of a child, or the quiet moments with loved ones.

This diversity in the search for meaning points to a fundamental truth: meaning is not something to be found but to be created. It's an active process, a daily decision to invest our time, energy, and heart into what matters most to us. It's about aligning our actions with our values, making choices that reflect what we believe necessary, and living in a way that brings a sense of fulfillment and satisfaction.

But here's the catch: searching for meaning is not a linear journey. It's fraught with challenges, setbacks, and moments of doubt. There will be times when the path is clear, and the sense of purpose is vital. But there will also be times when meaning seems elusive, our carefully laid plans crumble, and our questions outnumber our answers.

In these moments, in the heart of our suffering, our search for meaning is tested most profoundly.

Yet, it's also in these moments that we have the opportunity to deepen our understanding of what meaning truly is. Suffering, as much as we might wish to avoid it, can strip away the superficial, challenge our assumptions, and force us to reevaluate what is genuinely essential. It can catalyze growth, provide a doorway to more profound compassion, and remind us of our shared humanity.

So, what is meaning? It's a question that each of us must answer for ourselves, and the answer may change as we journey through life. However, one thing remains constant: the search for meaning, however we define it, makes us quintessentially human. It's a search that connects us, challenges us, and, ultimately, can lead us to a more prosperous, more fulfilling life.

Finding Purpose

Every person has a deep-seated desire to find purpose, a quest that often becomes more pronounced in the face of suffering. This journey can feel both daunting and exhilarating, leading us through paths both dark and light. But why is finding purpose so crucial, especially when grappling with the complexities of pain and hardship?

Purpose is our compass, guiding us through life's storms and calms. It gives our suffering a context, transforming it from a series of random events into a narrative we can understand and learn from. This doesn't mean that finding purpose is a cure-all for our woes—it's far from it. But it provides a framework that can help us navigate our challenges with more grace and resilience.

Consider, for a moment, the story of a young woman who, after a devastating accident, found herself unable to pursue her passion for dance. Lost and adrift in a sea of despair, she struggled to find meaning in her pain. She rediscovered a sense of purpose when she began to use her experience to inspire and teach others how to find joy in movement, regardless of their physical limitations. Her suffering, while still a part of her story, became a source of strength and inspiration rather than a point of stagnation.

This transformation is not unique. Across cultures and throughout history, individuals have found profound purpose amid their suffering. It's a testament to the human spirit's resilience and innate desire to seek meaning in our experiences. But how does one begin this quest for purpose, especially when suffering is too heavy to bear?

The journey starts with introspection. It's about asking ourselves the hard questions: What values are most important to me? What brings me joy and fulfillment? How can I contribute to the world in a way that feels meaningful? These questions don't have easy answers, and that's okay. The search for purpose is not about finding quick solutions but about embarking on a lifelong journey of discovery and growth.

It's also about looking beyond ourselves. Often, our purpose is deeply intertwined with our connections to others. Our interactions with others can provide powerful insights into our purpose, whether through acts of kindness, service or simply being present for those around us. In giving of ourselves, we often find ourselves.

Finally, it's important to remember that our purpose can evolve over time. As we grow and change, so too can our understanding of what gives our life meaning. Embracing this fluidity can help us remain open to new possibilities, even in adversity.

Finding purpose in suffering is not about diminishing the pain or pretending it doesn't exist. It's about weaving our experiences, both good and bad, into a larger tapestry of meaning that enriches our lives and the lives of those around us. It's a journey that requires courage, reflection, and an open heart but can also lead to profound growth and fulfillment. So, as we navigate the complexities of suffering, let us also embrace the quest for purpose, knowing that it holds the key to transforming our pain into a source of strength and wisdom.

The Role of Faith and Spirituality

The quest for meaning often leads us to the doorstep of faith and spirituality. It's a journey as old as humanity, yet each experience is profoundly personal and unique in its contours and colors.

Although sometimes used interchangeably, faith and spirituality address different aspects of our quest. Faith, in its essence, is about trust and conviction in something beyond the empirical, often tied to religious beliefs and practices. Spirituality, on the other hand, leans toward a broader understanding of connection, purpose, and the essence of being, not necessarily anchored in the doctrines of organized religion.

Why do these elements play a pivotal role in our search for meaning, especially in the face of suffering? Let's delve into this intricate dance.

Imagine standing at the edge of an expansive cityscape at night, the distant hum of traffic whispering secrets of the universe. In this moment, you're confronted with the vastness of existence and your place within it. This is where faith and spirituality become skyscrapers, guiding us through the darkness. They offer a sense of belonging, a connection to something greater than ourselves, and a framework to understand the unfathomable complexities of life and suffering.

For many, faith provides a narrative that makes sense

of pain and loss. It offers hope, a promise of a larger plan, or a future where today's tears might find their resolution. It's a source of strength, a well to draw from when our reserves run dry. In the stories of faith—across religions and cultures—we find heroes and heroines who've traversed valleys of darkness and emerged transformed, not unscathed but undeniably stronger and more compassionate.

Spirituality, with its broader canopy, invites us to find meaning through connection—to the divine, each other, nature, and our inner selves. It encourages mindfulness, the art of living fully in the present, finding depth and significance in the now, even amidst turmoil. It teaches us about the impermanence of suffering, the ebb and flow of life's tides, and the growth that often sprouts from the soil of pain.

Yet, the journey is not without its challenges. Doubt, despair, and the feeling of abandonment can shadow the path. Here, the stories of faith and spiritual exploration become solace and mirrors reflecting our doubts and eventual breakthroughs. They remind us that the quest for meaning is not a solitary trek but a shared pilgrimage enriched by the wisdom and companionship of those who've walked before us.

In embracing faith and spirituality, we're not negating the reality of suffering or looking for an escape hatch. Instead, we're opening ourselves to a different perspective that sees suffering not as an end but as a passage, a crucible in which the true essence of life is refined and revealed.

As we navigate through the chapters of our own lives, the role of faith and spirituality in our search for meaning might evolve, shift shapes, or even take us by surprise. But at its core, it remains a testament to our enduring quest for light in the darkness, a song amidst the silence, and a sense of belonging in the vast, mysterious expanse of existence.

Meaning Through Work

The quest for meaning often leads us down various paths, with work being one of the most significant avenues through which we seek purpose and fulfillment. It's not just about earning a living or climbing the career ladder; it's about finding a more profound sense of value in what we do, contributing to something beyond ourselves, and, in the process, defining who we are.

For many, work is more than a job. It's a calling. It's where passion meets profession, and skills and interests align to create something meaningful. This alignment doesn't happen overnight or come without its share of challenges and setbacks. Yet, in the pursuit of this alignment, we often find our most profound lessons and rewards.

Consider the story of a teacher who finds joy in the

spark of understanding in her students' eyes or the carpenter who sees his soul in the furniture he crafts. Their work goes beyond the immediate tasks; it reflects their identity and contribution to the world. This is where work transcends the mundane and becomes a source of deep satisfaction and meaning.

However, finding meaning in work isn't reserved for those who've found their "dream jobs." It's also about perspective and mindset. Even in the most routine tasks, there's an opportunity to find significance. It could be in the relationships we build, the challenges we overcome, or the small victories we celebrate daily. It's about seeing the value in our contributions, no matter how small they seem.

But what happens when work feels more like a burden than a source of fulfillment? Many face this reality, and it's here that the concept of mindset comes into play. Viewing challenges as opportunities for growth, focusing on what can be learned from difficult situations, and finding small ways to inject passion into our work can transform our experience. This shift in perspective doesn't just change how we view our work; it changes how we experience life.

In essence, meaning through work is as much about what we bring to it as what we take away. It's a dynamic interplay between our skills, our passions, and the opportunities we're given. It's about making the most of what we have while always striving for what sets our hearts on fire. In this pursuit, we not only enrich our lives but also the lives of those around us, creating a ripple effect of purpose and passion.

So, as we navigate the complexities of finding meaning through work, let's remember that it's not just about the destination but also the journey. It's about the lessons learned, the relationships forged, and the small moments of joy and satisfaction. Ultimately, these experiences weave the rich tapestry of a well-lived life filled with purpose and meaning.

Contributing to Others

In our journey through life, we often find ourselves grappling with suffering. It's a universal experience that touches every human being on this planet in one way or another. But amidst the trials and tribulations, there lies a profound opportunity for growth and meaning—especially when we turn our gaze outward towards contributing to the lives of others.

Contributing to others can take myriad forms, from simple acts of kindness to grand gestures of philanthropy. Yet, the essence remains the same: it's about extending ourselves beyond our personal boundaries, reaching out to touch the lives of others in positive ways. This act, as simple as it may seem, holds the power to transform not just the lives of those we help but also our own lives.

Consider the story of Anna, a woman who felt a deep

despair and worthlessness after losing her job. The future seemed bleak, and her place in the world was uncertain. During this dark period, she decided to volunteer at a local food bank. Initially, her decision was driven by a desire to fill her time and, perhaps, to find a distraction from her own troubles. However, something within her shifted as she began to immerse herself in the work. She saw the direct impact of her efforts on the lives of those who came to the food bank—families who could now enjoy a meal and children who smiled a little brighter. This experience brought a new sense of purpose and meaning to her life. Anna realized that her value was not tied to her job or status but to her ability to make a difference in the lives of others.

This story illustrates a powerful truth: when we contribute to the well-being of others, we not only alleviate their suffering but also find a pathway out of our own. It's a reciprocal relationship, where the giver often receives as much, if not more, than the recipient. This act of giving and contributing becomes a source of meaning and fulfillment, a beacon of light in our journey through suffering.

Moreover, contributing to others helps us to cultivate a sense of connectedness and belonging. It reminds us that we are not isolated islands of existence but part of a larger, interconnected community. This realization can be incredibly healing, especially in moments of personal suffering. It provides a sense of perspective, a reminder that our struggles are part of the human condition and that by helping others, we are, in a way, helping ourselves.

In essence, contributing to others is a powerful antidote to suffering. It offers a path toward finding meaning and purpose in our lives, even in adversity. It teaches us that we can make a difference even when we feel most powerless. And most importantly, it shows us that we find our true selves by giving.

Chapter Summary

- Meaning in life is deeply personal, evolving, and unique, encompassing the significance, value, and purpose we find.
- People find meaning through various pursuits such as knowledge, art, service, or the simplicity of life, highlighting the diversity in the search for meaning.
- The search for meaning is an active, daily decision that involves aligning actions with values and living in a way that brings fulfillment.
- Suffering tests the search for meaning and offers opportunities to deepen understanding

and growth, showing the importance of resilience and perspective.
- Finding purpose, especially in suffering, serves as a compass, providing context and a narrative to our experiences, and can lead to growth and fulfillment.
- Faith and spirituality play pivotal roles in the quest for meaning, offering belonging, hope, and a framework to understand life's complexities.
- Work is a significant avenue for finding meaning, where passion meets profession, and even routine tasks can offer significance through perspective and mindset.
- Contributing to others alleviates not only their suffering but also our own, fostering a sense of connectedness and belonging and being a powerful path to finding meaning.

8

THE BODY-MIND CONNECTION

Physical Health and Mental Well-being

In life, the connection between our physical health and mental well-being often takes center stage, yet we sometimes overlook its significance. It's a relationship that's as complex as it is crucial, influencing how we feel on any given day and shaping our overall quality of life. This section delves into the profound interplay between the body and mind, exploring how nurturing one benefits the other and vice versa.

Let's start with a simple truth: our bodies and minds are not separate entities. They are parts of a whole, constantly communicating in a language we're just beginning to understand. When our physical health suffers, it sends ripples through our mental state, affecting our mood, energy levels, and even our perception of the world. Conversely, mental stress can manifest physically, leading to a host of issues ranging from sleep disturbances to chronic diseases.

I remember a period when I was juggling tight deadlines at work with personal challenges. My stress levels were through the roof, and unsurprisingly, my health took a nosedive. I caught every cold going around, felt perpetually tired, and my usual upbeat mindset was nowhere to be found. It was a stark reminder of how closely our mental and physical states are intertwined.

Research backs this up, showing that regular physical activity can significantly reduce symptoms of depression and anxiety. Exercise releases endorphins, often dubbed 'feel-good' hormones, which can lift our spirits and provide a sense of well-being. But it's not just about hitting the gym or running marathons; even gentle, regular movement like walking or yoga can make a difference.

Nutrition, too, plays a pivotal role. The food we consume can influence our brain's structure and function, affecting our mood and energy levels. A diet rich in fruits, vegetables, lean proteins, and whole grains can help fend off feelings of depression and anxiety. In contrast, a diet high in processed foods and sugar can exacerbate them.

Sleep is another critical piece of the puzzle. Quality sleep helps regulate mood, improve brain function, and strengthen the immune system. On the flip side, sleep deprivation can lead to irritability, increased stress, and a host of mental health issues.

But here's the good news: improving our physical health—whether through exercise, nutrition or getting enough sleep—can significantly boost our mental well-being. It's a virtuous cycle: caring for our body enriches our mind, and nurturing our mental health enhances our physical state.

The journey towards a healthier, happier life begins with recognizing and respecting the body-mind connection. It's about making conscious choices that benefit our physical and mental health, leading to a more balanced, fulfilling life. As we continue to explore this connection, we unlock the potential to survive and thrive, even in the face of suffering.

The Impact of Nutrition

When we talk about the body-mind connection, the role of nutrition cannot be overstated. It's fascinating how the food we eat can profoundly impact our mental well-being, shaping our mindset and, in turn, our experience of suffering.

Let's dive into this a bit. Imagine your body as a finely tuned machine. Like any machine, the quality of fuel you put into it significantly affects its performance. In the context of our bodies, the fuel is the food we consume.

High-quality, nutrient-rich foods can enhance mental clarity, mood, and overall health. At the same time, a diet lacking essential nutrients can lead to many problems, including increased susceptibility to stress and a negative mindset.

Consider, for example, omega-3 fatty acids' role in foods like fish, flaxseeds, and walnuts. Research has shown that these fats are crucial for brain health, influencing mood and cognitive function. A deficiency in omega-3s has been linked to higher levels of depression and anxiety. It's a clear example of how our dietary choices impact our mental state.

Similarly, the gut-brain axis presents another compelling case for the impact of nutrition on our mindset. The gut is often called the "second brain" because of the vast network of neurons lining our gastrointestinal tract. This "second brain" communicates with our actual brain, influencing our emotions and mental state. A diet rich in probiotics and fiber supports a healthy gut microbiome, which, in turn, supports a healthy mind. It's a symbiotic relationship that underscores the importance of nutrition in managing our mental well-being.

But it's not just about individual nutrients. The overall quality of our diet plays a crucial role in our mental health. Diets high in processed foods, sugar, and unhealthy fats can exacerbate feelings of anxiety and depression, making it harder to cope with stress and suffering. Conversely, a balanced diet rich in fruits, vegetables, whole grains, lean protein, and healthy fats can foster a more positive mindset, making us more resilient in life's challenges.

In my own journey, I've seen the transformative power of nutrition firsthand. There was a time when my diet was poor, and my mental health suffered for it. I was irritable and anxious and struggled to find joy in life. It wasn't until I made a conscious effort to improve my diet, focusing on whole, nutrient-rich foods, that I noticed a significant shift in my mindset. I became more positive, resilient, and equipped to handle stress and suffering.

So, as we navigate the complex terrain of mindset and suffering, let's pay attention to the foundational role of nutrition. By making mindful choices about what we eat, we can support our mental health and cultivate a mindset that empowers us to face life's challenges with strength and grace. It's a simple yet profound step we can all take toward a healthier, happier life.

Exercise and Mental Health

In mental health, the power of exercise is often overshadowed by more traditional approaches like therapy and medication. Yet, the link between physical activity and psychological well-being is undeniable and profound. It's not just about the endorphins; those chemicals are often touted as nature's mood lifters. The benefits of exercise delve deeper, touching on aspects of our mental health that can transform our approach to suffering and our mindset towards it.

Consider the feeling of accomplishment after a run, the meditative state achieved during a yoga session, or the simple joy of a leisurely walk in the park. These experiences do more than improve our physical health; they offer a respite for our minds, a momentary escape from the clutches of our worries and stresses. Exercise, in its many forms, acts as a natural combatant against the symptoms of anxiety and depression, offering a buffer of resilience we can build upon.

But how does this work? When we move our bodies, we're not just working our muscles but also engaging our minds. Regular physical activity can help regulate our sleep patterns, improve our self-esteem, and provide control over our bodies and, by extension, our lives. It's a way of signaling to ourselves that we can effect change, both externally and internally. This sense of agency is crucial when navigating the murky waters of suffering and mental health challenges.

Moreover, exercise fosters a sense of community. Whether it's joining a local sports team, attending group fitness classes, or simply walking with a friend, these activities connect us with others. They remind us that we're not alone in our struggles, providing a support network that can be invaluable during tough times.

Yet, it's essential to approach exercise with self-compassion and understanding. The goal isn't to run a marathon or achieve a particular physique but to find activities that bring joy and comfort. It's about moving your body in good and beneficial ways, not punishing yourself for not meeting arbitrary standards.

Exercise can be a powerful tool for managing mental health in the context of suffering. It offers a way to directly influence our mindset, providing a sense of control and accomplishment. By incorporating physical activity into our lives, we can build a foundation of mental and physical resilience that supports us in facing challenges and overcoming obstacles.

So, let's lace up our sneakers, unroll our yoga mats, or take a moment to stretch. Let's remind ourselves that our bodies and minds are intrinsically linked, and by nurturing one, we nurture the other. In the journey towards overcoming suffering and fostering a positive mindset, exercise is a companion worth having by our side.

Sleep and Recovery

Sleep often gets relegated to the background, a necessity we try to squeeze between our bustling days and endless to-do lists. Yet, as we delve deeper into the body-mind connection, we uncover the profound impact of sleep on our mental well-being, ability to cope with suffering, and overall mindset.

Imagine sleep as the silent healer, working its magic as we drift into oblivion. During these precious hours, our bodies embark on a meticulous repair and rejuvenation process while our minds sort through the day's experiences, consolidating memories and processing emotions. This isn't just about getting rest; it's about allowing ourselves to recover and heal from the stresses and strains that life invariably throws our way.

Consider the nights when sleep eludes you, when you toss and turn, haunted by worries or replaying scenarios that left you feeling drained. The next day feels like an uphill battle. Your mood might take a hit, your patience wears thin, and that inner resilience seems just out of reach. This isn't a coincidence but a testament to the intricate link between our sleep patterns and mental state.

But here's the good news: prioritizing sleep can enhance our ability to navigate life's challenges with grace. It's akin to equipping ourselves with stronger armor against the slings and arrows of outrageous fortune. A well-rested mind is more adaptable, capable of finding silver linings, and more resilient in adversity. It's about setting the stage for a positive mindset that can transform suffering into a source of growth and learning.

So, how do we harness the power of sleep in our quest for a healthier mindset? It starts with recognizing sleep as a non-negotiable pillar of self-care. Create a sleep sanctuary, a space that invites tranquility and relaxation. Establish a routine that signals to your body it's time to wind down, whether through reading, meditation, or gentle stretches. And perhaps most importantly, listen to your body. When it whispers its need for rest, heed its call.

Sleep is a chapter we cannot afford to skip in the narrative of overcoming suffering and cultivating a resilient mindset. It's the foundation upon which we build our strength, optimism, and capacity to thrive in life's inevitable challenges. Let's not underestimate the power of a good night's sleep; it might be the key to unlocking a more resilient, joyful self.

Stress Management

Stress has become a constant, unwelcome companion in the hustle and bustle of our daily lives. It's like that one guest at a party who overstays their welcome, draining our energy and leaving us feeling depleted. But here's the thing: managing stress isn't just about finding ways to relax; it's about understanding the intricate dance between our minds and bodies and how one influences the other.

Let's start with a simple truth: our bodies react to stress in ways meant to protect us. Think of it as your body's alarm system. When you perceive a threat, your body releases hormones, including adrenaline and cortisol, which prepare you to fight or flee. This was incredibly useful back when our ancestors had to dodge saber-toothed tigers. Still, this physiological response can become chronic in our modern world, wreaking havoc on our well-being.

The impact of prolonged stress on the body is profound. It can lead to a myriad of health issues, including heart disease, diabetes, and a weakened immune system. But here's where it gets interesting: just as the body affects the mind, the mind can influence the body. By adopting specific mental strategies, we can mitigate the physical effects of stress.

Mindfulness and meditation are powerful tools in this regard. They teach us to stay present, observing our thoughts and feelings without judgment. This practice can help lower cortisol levels, reducing the physical symptoms of stress. Similarly, cognitive-behavioral strategies can change how we perceive stressors, effectively reducing the volume of our body's alarm system.

Exercise, too, plays a crucial role in stress management. It's not just about keeping fit; physical activity releases endorphins, chemicals in the brain that act as natural painkillers and mood elevators. Regular exercise can help you maintain a sense of calm. It can counteract the adverse effects of stress on your body.

Let's remember the power of connection. Building solid and supportive relationships can provide a buffer against stress. Knowing you have someone to turn to can make all the difference when facing challenging times.

Incorporating these strategies into your life doesn't mean stress will magically disappear. But it does mean you'll be better equipped to handle whatever comes your way. Think of it as tuning your body's instrument; when mind and body are in harmony, you're more resilient and capable of facing life's ups and downs.

So, as we navigate the complexities of our world, let's remember the profound connection between our minds and bodies. By nurturing both, we can transform our relationship with stress, turning it from a formidable foe into a manageable part of our lives. After all, it's not the presence of stress that defines our experience but how we respond to it.

Chapter Summary

- The body-mind connection is crucial for overall quality of life, with physical health and mental well-being deeply intertwined.
- Physical ailments can affect mental state, and mental stress can manifest physically, impacting overall health.

- Regular physical activity reduces symptoms of depression and anxiety, with exercise releasing endorphins that improve mood.
- Nutrition plays a significant role in mental health, with a balanced diet improving mood and energy. In contrast, poor diets can worsen mental health issues.
- Quality sleep is essential for mental well-being, regulating mood, improving brain function, and strengthening the immune system.
- Improving physical health through exercise, nutrition, and sleep can boost mental well-being, creating a virtuous cycle.
- Stress management is critical, and mindfulness, meditation, and exercise effectively mitigate the physical effects of stress.

9

THE SCIENCE OF HAPPINESS

Understanding Happiness

Happiness is a concept as elusive as it is sought after. In our quest to understand it, we often find ourselves tangled in a web of scientific theories, philosophical debates, and personal reflections. Yet, at its core, happiness is a deeply personal experience shaped by our mindset, circumstances, and, perhaps surprisingly, our encounters with suffering.

Let's start with a simple truth: happiness is not constant. It ebbs and flows, influenced by many factors ranging from genetic predispositions to the quality of our relationships. This fluidity makes happiness so intriguing and sometimes frustrating to pin down. It's akin to trying to hold water in your hands; the tighter you grasp, the quicker it seems to slip through your fingers.

Science has made strides in demystifying happiness, highlighting the importance of a positive mindset and resilience in adversity. Individuals who can find meaning in their suffering and view challenges as growth opportunities often report higher levels of life satisfaction. This doesn't mean that suffering is a prerequisite for happiness, but rather that how we respond to life's inevitable hardships can significantly influence our overall well-being.

On a personal note, I recall a period in my life when everything was falling apart. During this time, amidst the chaos and uncertainty, I stumbled upon a profound realization: happiness was not about the absence of suffering but about the presence of hope and the ability to appreciate the small moments of joy that life offers, even in the darkest of times.

This realization brings us to another critical aspect of happiness: gratitude. Cultivating gratitude, even for the most mundane aspects of our lives, can shift our focus from what we lack to what we possess. It's a simple yet powerful shift in perspective that can significantly enhance our happiness.

Moreover, the role of social connections must be balanced. Humans are inherently social beings, and our relationships are crucial in our pursuit of happiness. Firm, supportive relationships provide a buffer against the stresses of life, offering comfort, joy, and a sense of belonging.

In conclusion, understanding happiness requires us to look beyond the surface and explore the intricate interplay between our mindset, experiences, and connections with others. It's a journey that is as unique as it is universal, reminding us that happiness, in its many forms, is within reach, even when it feels just out of grasp.

Psychology of Happiness

Diving into the psychology of happiness, we find ourselves at the heart of a fascinating exploration. It's a journey that takes us beyond the surface of smiles and good moods into the deeper realms of our minds and how we perceive and interact with the world around us. As it turns out, happiness is not just a fleeting emotion or a momentary state of being. It's a complex psychological phenomenon deeply intertwined with our thoughts, beliefs, and behaviors.

At its core, the psychology of happiness revolves around subjective well-being. This encompasses more than just the absence of negative emotions—it's about the presence of positive emotions and a profound sense of satisfaction with life. It's the kind of happiness that lingers, buffering us against the challenges we face and enriching our daily experiences.

One of the most empowering aspects of this field is the discovery that our happiness is, to a significant extent, within our control. While genetics and life circumstances play a role, a large portion of our happiness is determined by our actions and mindset. This is where the concept of intentional activities comes into play. These are actions we can take deliberately to boost our happiness. Whether cultivating gratitude, engaging in acts of kindness, or setting and pursuing meaningful goals, these activities can improve our overall well-being.

Another key finding in the psychology of happiness is the importance of relationships. Strong, healthy relationships are one of the most significant predictors of happiness. It's not just about having people around us; it's about having deep, meaningful connections that provide support, love, and a sense of belonging. These connections act as a buffer against stress and are a source of joy and fulfillment in their own right.

Mindfulness and living in the moment also play a crucial role in our happiness. By being fully present and engaged with our current experiences, we can reduce the impact of negative thoughts and emotions. Mindfulness helps us appreciate the moment's beauty, leading to a more prosperous life.

Lastly, the psychology of happiness teaches us about hedonic adaptation—the idea that we quickly get used to changes in our circumstances, whether good or bad. This means that chasing after external sources of happiness, like material possessions or achievements, often leads to a temporary boost in happiness, followed by a return to our baseline level. Understanding this concept encourages us to seek happiness not in external achievements but in internal growth and cultivating positive experiences and relationships.

In essence, the psychology of happiness offers valuable insights into cultivating a more profound, more enduring sense of well-being. It's not about chasing after fleeting moments of joy but about building a rich life in meaning, connection, and contentment. As we navigate the complexities of our minds and the challenges of our lives, these insights can guide us toward a happier, more fulfilled existence.

Happiness and Health

In life, happiness and health strengthen one another in a vibrant display of well-being. It's a simple and profound concept: the happier we are, the healthier we tend to be. But how does this connection work, and why is it crucial to understand?

First, let's dive into the science. Studies have shown that happiness can lead to a plethora of health benefits. These range from the more obvious, like reduced stress levels, to the less apparent, such as a more robust immune system. When we're happy, our body's stress hormones, such as cortisol, decrease, allowing our immune cells to function more effectively. This doesn't just mean we're less likely to catch a cold; it also affects long-term health outcomes, reducing our risk of chronic diseases like heart disease.

Moreover, happiness directly influences our heart health. A positive outlook on life has been linked to lower blood pressure, reduced risk for heart disease, and improved heart rate variability. It's as if our happiness sends a signal to our heart, telling it to beat not just stronger but smarter.

But the benefits don't stop at the physical. Happiness also profoundly affects our mental health. It can act as a buffer against mental health challenges, making us more resilient to stress and reducing the risk of conditions like depression and anxiety. This resilience isn't just about feeling good at the moment; it's about building a foundation of mental strength that helps us navigate life's ups and downs.

The relationship between happiness and health is bidirectional. Just as happiness can lead to better health, improving our physical well-being can boost our mood and overall happiness. Regular exercise, a balanced diet, and sufficient sleep all contribute to this cycle of well-being, holistically enhancing our quality of life.

Understanding this connection is more than academic;

it's a call to action. It invites us to look at our lives and ask, "What makes me happy?" and "How can I incorporate more of that into my daily routine?" It's about recognizing that small, joyful moments—whether it's a morning walk, a chat with a friend, or simply taking a few deep breaths—can profoundly impact our health.

Pursuing happiness is not just a quest for a fleeting feeling. It's a journey towards a healthier, more fulfilled life. By embracing happiness, we're not just brightening our days; we're nurturing our bodies, fortifying our minds, and enriching our lives. So, let's not underestimate the power of a smile, the strength found in laughter, or the healing found in joy. After all, in the intricate dance of life, happiness and health move together, each step leading us closer to well-being.

Cultivating Joy

Joy often seems elusive in life, especially when navigating suffering and hardship. Yet, in these times, cultivating joy becomes not just a possibility but a necessity. The journey towards joy isn't about denying our suffering but learning to grow even amid storms. Let's explore how we can cultivate joy in our lives, drawing from the rich soil of our good and bad experiences.

Firstly, it's essential to recognize that joy doesn't always come from external circumstances. It often springs from within, from a mindset that chooses to find beauty in the mundane, strength in adversity, and opportunities in challenges. This doesn't mean we ignore our pain or pretend it doesn't exist. Instead, we acknowledge, learn from, and allow it to coexist with our moments of happiness. It's about finding balance, not pretending.

One practical way to cultivate joy is through gratitude. It sounds simple, perhaps even cliché, but acknowledging and appreciating what we have, rather than fixating on what we lack, can shift our entire perspective. Start small. It could be as simple as the warmth of the sun on your skin, a message from a friend, or the taste of your favorite food. Gratitude grounds us in the present moment, reminding us of the abundance surrounding us, even when it feels like we're drowning in scarcity.

Another pathway to joy is connection. Human beings are wired for connection; it's in our DNA. Isolation amplifies our suffering, while connection can be a balm for our wounds. Reach out, build relationships, and share your journey with others. Joy shared is joy multiplied. It's in the shared smiles, the laughter that bubbles up during conversations, and the comfort of knowing you're not alone in your struggles.

Let's remember the power of helping others. Acts of kindness and service bring joy not only to those we help but to ourselves as well. A profound happiness comes from making a difference in someone else's life, no matter how small. It reminds us of our own agency and our impact on the world around us.

Lastly, embrace the journey. Joy is not a destination but a way of traveling. It's found in the small moments, the lessons learned, and the growth that comes from overcoming. It's okay to simultaneously feel joy and sadness; it signifies a prosperous life. Cultivating joy doesn't mean we won't face more valleys of suffering. Still, it ensures we'll have the resilience, connections, and mindset to navigate them gracefully.

In the end, cultivating joy is an act of defiance against the darkness of suffering. It's a declaration that even in our lowest moments, we can find reasons to smile, to hope, and to keep moving forward. So, let's cultivate joy not as a fleeting emotion but as a state of being, a lens through which we view the world, even when that world seems clouded by suffering.

The Role of Gratitude

In human emotions, gratitude is one to recognize. Gratitude is more than just saying "thank you." It's a profound appreciation for what we have and the world around us, recognizing the good that exists despite challenges and suffering. It's a transformative force capable of shifting our mindset from scarcity to abundance, from despair to hope.

The science of happiness has increasingly turned its gaze towards understanding how gratitude functions as an emotion and practice. This habit can be cultivated to improve our mental and emotional well-being. Studies have shown that people who regularly practice gratitude report feeling happier, more satisfied with their lives, and less stressed. They tend to be more resilient in the face of adversity, viewing obstacles not as insurmountable barriers but as challenges to be overcome. This doesn't mean they ignore the negative aspects of life; instead, they focus on the positive, finding joy and meaning in the small, everyday moments.

But how does one cultivate gratitude, especially when suffering overshadows everything else? It starts with intention. Like planting a seed in fertile soil, we must first consciously seek out and acknowledge the good in our lives. This can be as simple as keeping a gratitude journal, where we jot down three daily things we're thankful for. Over time, this practice can shift our perspective, helping us to see the world in a new light.

I remember a period in my life when everything seemed to fall apart. It was a time of profound personal loss and uncertainty. Amid this darkness, I stumbled upon the idea of gratitude journaling. Skeptical but desperate for a lifeline, I began to write. Some days, it was as mundane as being thankful for a cup of coffee or a warm bed. On other days, it was the kindness of a friend or a moment of unexpected beauty. Slowly, almost imperceptibly, my outlook began to change. I noticed and appreciated the good more often, feeling lighter and more at peace even though my circumstances hadn't dramatically changed. This small practice became a beacon of hope, a reminder that even in our darkest hours, glimmers of light can be found.

Gratitude, then, is not just a feeling but a tool, a powerful antidote to suffering. It doesn't negate the pain or the challenges we face. Instead, it offers us a way to navigate through them, to find joy and meaning amid adversity. By choosing gratitude, we focus on the abundance in our lives to celebrate the good, and in doing so, we open ourselves up to a more profound, more fulfilling experience of happiness.

Sustainable Happiness

In our quest for happiness, we often stumble upon the question: How can we make it last? It's one thing to experience fleeting moments of joy. Still, it is quite another to cultivate a sense of happiness that endures through the ups and downs of life. This is where the concept of sustainable happiness comes into play. It's not just about chasing after pleasurable experiences or avoiding pain at all costs. Instead, it's about building a foundation of well-being that can sustain us even when times get tough.

Sustainable happiness is rooted in our approach to life. It's about adopting a mindset that values growth, resilience, and a deep sense of purpose. It involves recognizing that happiness is not a destination to be reached but a journey that unfolds moment by moment. Crucially, it's about understanding that our happiness is interconnected with the well-being of others and the world around us.

One key aspect of sustainable happiness is cultivating gratitude. As discussed in the previous section, when we take time to appreciate what we have rather than constantly yearning for more, we open ourselves to a more profound sense of contentment. Gratitude shifts our focus from what's missing to the already present abundance. It's a simple practice, but its effects can be profound.

Another critical component is the pursuit of meaningful activities. Engaging in work or hobbies that align with our values and passions brings a sense of fulfillment that superficial pleasures can't match. When we lose ourselves in activities that matter to us, we experience a state of flow where time seems to stand still, and our worries fade away. This is happiness at its most pure and sustainable.

Of course, the journey towards sustainable happiness has its challenges. Life will inevitably throw curveballs, testing our resilience and forcing us to adapt. But in these moments of struggle, the value of happiness built on solid ground becomes apparent. By embracing adversity as an opportunity for growth, we can emerge stronger and more content than before.

In the end, sustainable happiness is not a one-size-fits-all formula. It's a deeply personal endeavor that requires us to look inward and ask ourselves what truly brings us joy. It invites us to let go of societal pressures and external measures of success and instead chart our own path to well-being. And while the journey may be long and winding, the rewards are well worth the effort. After all, what could be more fulfilling than a life filled with genuine, lasting happiness?

Chapter Summary

- Happiness is a fluid and profoundly personal experience influenced by mindset, circumstances, and responses to suffering.
- Scientific research highlights the importance of a positive mindset and resilience, suggesting that finding meaning in suffering can enhance life satisfaction.
- Gratitude and strong social connections play crucial roles in achieving happiness, shifting focus from what we lack to what we possess, and providing support and belonging.

- The psychology of happiness delves into subjective well-being, emphasizing control over happiness through intentional activities, the significance of relationships, and mindfulness.
- Happiness contributes to physical and mental health by reducing stress, strengthening the immune system, and buffering against mental health challenges.
- Cultivating joy involves recognizing internal sources of happiness, practicing gratitude, fostering connections, and embracing the journey with balance and resilience.
- Gratitude, as a practice, can transform our perspective from scarcity to abundance, enhancing mental and emotional well-being even in the face of adversity.
- Sustainable happiness focuses on growth, purpose, and interconnected well-being, advocating for gratitude, meaningful activities, and resilience against life's challenges.

10

RESILIENCE IN THE FACE OF ADVERSITY

What is Resilience?

Resiliency is at the heart of our journey through the landscape of mindset and suffering. It's a term we often hear, especially in the context of overcoming challenges and adversities. But what exactly is resilience? Let's explore its nuances and why it's crucial in our lives.

Resilience, in its essence, is the capacity to bounce back from difficulties. It's about facing life's storms and emerging intact and perhaps even stronger than before. This doesn't mean that resilient people don't experience stress, emotional upheaval, or suffering. Quite the contrary. Resilience involves experiencing these challenges deeply but not letting them define or debilitate you.

Think of resilience as a muscle. Just as physical

exercise strengthens the body, navigating through challenges and adversities strengthens resilience. It's not an innate trait that only a lucky few possess. Instead, it's a skill that can be developed, honed, and nurtured over time. This is an empowering realization because it means that there's always room to grow our resilience no matter where we are on our journey.

Why is resilience so important? Life, as we know, is unpredictable. It throws curveballs when we least expect them. In these moments, resilience helps us adapt, persevere, and ultimately overcome the obstacles we face. It enables us to keep moving forward, even when the path is steep and the night is dark.

Resilience also plays a crucial role in our overall well-being. It's linked to lower rates of depression, higher levels of satisfaction with life, and a greater sense of meaning and purpose. In other words, resilience doesn't just help us survive; it helps us thrive.

But how do we build resilience? It starts with our mindset. Viewing challenges as opportunities for growth, maintaining a positive outlook, and practicing self-compassion are all critical components. It also involves connecting with others, seeking support when needed, and giving support in return. No matter how small, each step we take builds upon the last, creating a foundation of strength and resilience.

As we continue our exploration of mindset and

suffering, remember that resilience is not a destination but a journey. It's not about never falling but about learning how to rise each time we do. And in this journey, we're not alone. Together, we can navigate the challenges, learn from them, and emerge stronger on the other side.

Building Resilience

Building resilience isn't just about bouncing back from adversity but growing through it. Imagine resilience as a muscle. Just as muscles become stronger through exercise, our resilience strengthens each time we face and navigate through difficulties. This process takes time and effort. It requires patience, effort, and a mindset willing to embrace challenges as opportunities for growth.

Firstly, understanding that resilience is not an innate trait but a skill that can be developed is crucial. It's easy to look at others who gracefully navigate hardships and think they're naturally resilient. However, resilience is often cultivated behind the scenes through consistent practice and a commitment to personal development.

One effective way to build resilience is by fostering a positive mindset. This doesn't mean ignoring the reality of a situation or pretending everything is fine when it's not. Instead, it's about maintaining a hopeful outlook and focusing on what you can control. It's about asking yourself, "What can I learn from this?" instead of "Why is this happening to me?" This shift in perspective can make a significant difference in how you approach challenges.

Another critical aspect is building a solid support network. Humans are social creatures, and having a community or even just a few trusted individuals to lean on can provide immense comfort and strength during tough times. These connections offer emotional support, practical advice, and sometimes just a listening ear, all of which are invaluable when navigating through adversity.

Self-care is also a vital component of resilience. It's tough to face challenges when you're already depleted. Ensuring you care for your physical, emotional, and mental health sets a strong foundation for resilience. This means getting enough sleep, eating well, staying active, and engaging in activities that bring you joy and relaxation.

Lastly, embracing failure as part of the learning process is essential. Every setback or failure is an opportunity to learn, grow, and adapt. Instead of viewing them as insurmountable obstacles, see them as stepping stones towards your goals. This mindset builds resilience and fosters a sense of perseverance and determination.

In summary, building resilience is a multifaceted process that involves developing a positive mindset, nurturing supportive relationships, practicing self-care, and learning from failure. It's a journey of personal growth that empowers you to face life's challenges with confidence and grace. Remember, resilience isn't about never falling; it's about how you get back up and what you learn in the process.

Resilience in Action

Resilience isn't just a buzzword; it's a lifeline. It's what separates those who can weather the storms of life from those who find themselves swept away by circumstances. But how does resilience manifest in real life? Let's dive into the heart of resilience in action, exploring how this powerful trait can transform suffering into strength.

Imagine facing a situation that seems impossible. It could be the loss of a loved one, a career setback, or a health crisis. These moments test our mettle, pushing us to the brink. Yet, it's precisely in these moments that resilience shines brightest. It's not about avoiding pain or suffering; it's about facing it head-on, acknowledging the hurt, and finding a way to move forward.

Resilience in action is about adaptability. It's recognizing that while we may not control every aspect of our lives, we control how we respond. This means taking a step back, assessing the situation, and deciding on the best action. Sometimes, it's about seeking support from friends, family, or professionals. Other times, it's about tapping into our inner resources, reminding ourselves of our strengths and past victories.

One of the most compelling aspects of resilience is its ability to foster growth. When we navigate adversity, we're not just surviving but learning. Each challenge teaches us something new about ourselves and the world around us. We discover hidden strengths, develop new skills, and sincerely appreciate life's blessings. This growth mindset is a critical component of resilience, turning obstacles into opportunities for personal development.

Moreover, resilience is contagious. When we model resilience in our own lives, we inspire those around us to do the same. It creates a ripple effect, building stronger individuals and communities. By sharing our stories of overcoming adversity, we offer hope and encouragement to others facing similar challenges. This collective resilience is a powerful force capable of transforming not just individual lives but society.

In essence, resilience in action is about embracing life's challenges with courage, grace, and determination. It's about knowing that the sun will rise again no matter how dark the night is. And with each new day comes the opportunity to grow stronger, wiser, and more resilient. So, let's celebrate resilience in all its forms, recognizing it as the invaluable asset it truly is in our journey through life.

Overcoming Trauma

Trauma is a formidable opponent. It sneaks up on us, often when we least expect it, leaving a trail of emotional and psychological upheaval. Yet, within the heart of this turmoil lies a seed of potential—a chance for growth and transformation. Overcoming trauma isn't about forgetting or erasing the past; it's about weaving our experiences into the fabric of who we are, becoming stronger and more resilient.

Imagine trauma as a powerful storm. It can uproot trees, destroy homes, and change landscapes forever. In the aftermath, the community comes together, clearing the debris and rebuilding, often with stronger materials and better foundations. Similarly, when we face our traumas, we can rebuild ourselves, not to be the same as before but stronger and more resilient.

The journey of overcoming trauma begins with acknowledgment. It's about facing the reality of our experiences, no matter how painful. This step is crucial and often the hardest. It requires courage to confront our vulnerabilities and the emotions tied to them. But remember, acknowledgment is not a sign of weakness; it's a brave step towards healing.

Next comes the process of understanding. Trauma can be confusing, leaving us with a tangled mess of emotions and questions. By seeking to understand our trauma, we embark on a path of self-discovery. This might involve therapy, journaling, or deep conversations with trusted friends or family. The goal is not to find a neat resolution but to gain insights into our feelings and reactions, which can be incredibly empowering.

Healing from trauma is not a linear process. There will be setbacks and days when the pain feels insurmountable. But it's important to remember that healing takes time and patience. It's okay to have bad days. What matters is that we keep moving forward, even if it's just one small step at a time.

One of the most powerful tools in overcoming trauma is connection. Isolation can amplify our pain, making it feel even more overwhelming. We remind ourselves that we're not alone by reaching out to others, whether through support groups, friends, or family. These connections provide comfort, understanding, and a sense of belonging, vital for healing.

Finally, transforming trauma involves finding meaning in our experiences. This doesn't mean viewing trauma as a "gift" or something to be grateful for. Instead, it's about asking ourselves how our experiences have shaped us and what we can learn from them. For many, this leads to a deeper appreciation for life, stronger relationships, and a newfound sense of purpose.

Overcoming trauma is a deeply personal journey, and there's no one-size-fits-all approach. It's about finding what works for you, whether that's through art, nature, spirituality, or any other form of expression that resonates with your soul. Remember, you're not defined by your trauma. You're defined by how you rise after falling, how you heal, and how you grow.

In the end, resilience isn't just about surviving; it's about thriving. It's about taking our broken pieces and putting them back together to make us stronger, wiser, and more compassionate. So, let's embrace our healing journey, knowing that on the other side of trauma, there's a world of possibility waiting for us.

The Role of Forgiveness

Forgiveness is a powerful tool in the journey toward resilience. It's not just about letting someone else off the hook for their actions or words; it's about freeing yourself from the weight of resentment and bitterness that can hold you back. When discussing forgiveness in the context of adversity, it's crucial to understand that it's a process, not a one-time event. It's a journey that can lead to profound healing and growth.

Imagine carrying a backpack filled with stones, each representing a grievance or hurt you've experienced. Over time, that backpack becomes heavier, making it harder to move forward. Forgiveness is taking those stones out, one by one, lightening your load and making the journey ahead less burdensome. It doesn't mean you forget the hurt or pretend it never happened. Instead, it means you no longer choose to let it control your life.

Forgiving doesn't necessarily mean reconciling with the person who hurt you. Sometimes, it's not possible or healthy to re-establish a relationship. Forgiveness is more about your inner peace and well-being. It's about taking back your power and not allowing someone else's actions to define you or your future.

The role of forgiveness in building resilience cannot be overstated. Resilient individuals often possess the ability to forgive, not because they are weak, but because they understand the strength and freedom that forgiveness brings. It allows them to overcome their pain and build a positive future. It's a crucial step in overcoming trauma and adversity.

Forgiveness also has a profound impact on our physical and mental health. Holding onto anger and resentment can lead to increased stress, affecting our immune system, sleep patterns, and overall well-being. By forgiving, we can reduce our stress levels and improve our health.

But how do you forgive when the hurt runs deep? It starts with acknowledging your pain and allowing yourself to feel it. It's okay to grieve the hurt. Then, when you're ready, you can consciously decide to let go of the anger and resentment. This involves understanding the context of the other person's actions, recognizing that we all make mistakes, or deciding that your peace is more important than holding onto the pain.

Forgiveness is a deeply personal process, and it looks different for everyone. It might involve writing a letter (that you never send), talking to a trusted friend or therapist, or practicing mindfulness and meditation to release your feelings. The key is to find what works for you and to be patient with yourself. Forgiveness takes time.

In the end, forgiveness is a gift you give yourself. It's an act of self-love and compassion that can transform your suffering into strength. It's a crucial step to resilience, allowing you to face adversity with a lighter heart and a clearer mind. Remember, the journey of forgiveness is not about reaching a destination; it's about finding freedom and peace along the way.

Chapter Summary

- Resilience is the capacity to recover quickly from difficulties and face life's challenges without being overwhelmed.
- It is not an innate trait but a skill that can be developed by facing adversities, akin to muscle strengthening.

- Resilience is crucial for adapting to life's unpredictability, contributing to lower depression rates, higher life satisfaction, and a greater sense of purpose.
- Building resilience involves adopting a positive mindset, viewing challenges as growth opportunities, and fostering supportive relationships.
- Self-care and learning from failures are also critical components of resilience, helping individuals navigate adversity more effectively.
- Resilience in action involves adaptability, learning from challenges, using personal strengths to overcome difficult situations, and fostering personal and community growth.
- Overcoming trauma requires acknowledging the pain, understanding the experience, connecting with others, and finding meaning in the adversity.
- Forgiveness, both of oneself and others is a vital step towards resilience. It allows individuals to move forward without being held back by past grievances.

11

THE ART OF LETTING GO

Understanding Attachment

At the heart of our journey through life, we often find ourselves clinging to various things: people, possessions, beliefs, and even past experiences. This clinging, or attachment, is a natural human tendency. It's how we make sense of the world, define ourselves, and seek security in an ever-changing universe. Yet, it's also a source of much of our suffering. Understanding attachment is the first step in mastering the art of letting go.

Attachment isn't inherently bad. It forms the basis of our relationships, fuels our passions, and drives us to achieve. However, when our happiness becomes overly dependent on something external—something we might lose—we set ourselves up for suffering. The fear of loss, the anxiety over change, and the pain of eventual separation can overshadow the joy of the present moment.

Consider for a moment the things to which you're most attached. It could be a person, a career, or a dream. Now, think about the emotions that arise when you imagine losing these attachments. Often, we'll find a mix of fear, sadness, and even anger. These feelings are signals pointing to our deep-seated attachments.

The process of letting go doesn't mean we must abandon our relationships, aspirations, or values. Instead, it's about loosening the grip of dependency we place on them for our inner peace and happiness. It's recognizing that while these things contribute to our joy, our essence and well-being don't solely depend on them.

As we navigate through the chapters of this book, we'll explore various strategies to cultivate a mindset that embraces letting go. From mindfulness practices that ground us in the present to cognitive shifts that reframe our perceptions of loss and change, the path is rich with opportunities for growth and transformation.

Letting go doesn't happen overnight. It's a practice, a daily choice to release the need for control and to trust in the flow of life. It's about finding freedom in the realization that our true happiness and peace come from within, not from the external world. This realization is liberating, opening us to a life of deeper meaning, joy, and connection.

The Process of Letting Go

Letting go is a journey, not a destination. It's a process that unfolds in its own time, a path we walk with patience and courage. The act of letting go is profoundly personal and varies from one individual to another. Yet, at its core, it involves steps that can guide us through the murky waters of attachment and lead us toward a place of peace and acceptance.

The first step in letting go is acknowledgment. It's about recognizing the emotions, attachments, and desires that bind us. This step requires honesty and bravery, as it often means facing parts of ourselves that we'd rather keep hidden. Acknowledgment is not about judgment; it's about seeing things as they are, without the filters of denial or wishful thinking.

Following acknowledgment, the next step is understanding. This involves delving deeper into the nature of our attachments. Why do we hold on so tightly? What fears are associated with letting go? Understanding our attachments gives us insight into our deeper selves and the patterns that govern our lives. It's a crucial step that paves the way for change.

Acceptance comes next. Acceptance doesn't mean agreement or resignation but recognizing that some things are beyond our control. It's about embracing our current reality, imperfections, and challenges. Acceptance is a powerful self-compassion that frees us from the struggle against what is.

With acceptance, we can move into the heart of letting go: release. Release is an act of trust. It's trusting that we can endure losing what we're attached to and find fulfillment and meaning without it. Release often involves a period of grief as we mourn what we've let go of. Yet, it's also a time of liberation as we free ourselves from the weight of our attachments.

The final step in the process of letting go is transformation. We open ourselves to new possibilities as we release our hold on the past. Transformation is about growth and renewal. It's about discovering who we can become when not defined by our attachments. This step is not the journey's end but a new beginning, a gateway to a more freedom and authentic life.

The process of letting go is not linear. We may find ourselves revisiting steps or experiencing them in a different order. What's important is to keep moving forward, even when the path is unclear. Letting go is a practice, a choice we make again and again. It's a commitment to our well-being and growth, a testament to our strength and resilience.

As we navigate the process of letting go, we learn it's not just about releasing what no longer serves us. It's also about embracing what comes next. It's about living fully in the present and opening our hearts to the future. Letting go is an art, one that we refine over a lifetime. In this art, we find the end of suffering and the beginning of true freedom.

Forgiveness and Release

Forgiveness and release are towering milestones in personal growth and healing on the journey towards inner peace. It's not just about letting go of the past but also about freeing ourselves from the chains of resentment and bitterness that can hold us back from living fully in the present.

Forgiveness is more for us than it is for those who have wronged us. It's a gift we give ourselves—a declaration that we are no longer willing to carry the weight of someone else's mistakes. But let's be clear, forgiving is not synonymous with forgetting or condoning. It doesn't mean you must welcome someone back into your life with open arms or pretend that what they did was acceptable. It means you're choosing to release the grip of anger and resentment on your heart.

The process of forgiveness and release often begins with acknowledging the pain. It's okay to admit that you're hurt. It's okay to feel angry. These emotions are not signs of weakness but of being human. The key is to keep them from becoming your permanent residence. Like clouds in the sky, let them pass. This only happens after some time.

It's a journey, sometimes long, but every step forward lightens the load.

Release is about letting go of the narratives we've built around our pain. It's about stopping the endless loop of hurtful memories and what-ifs that play in our minds. This is where the art of mindfulness can be compelling. By bringing our attention to the present moment, we can gently start to detach from those stories that keep us anchored to our past. It's about recognizing that we have the power to write new stories, ones that are rooted in forgiveness, growth, and hope.

One of the most profound realizations on this journey is that forgiveness and release are acts of self-love. They are acknowledgments of our own worth and a testament to our strength and resilience. By forgiving, we honor ourselves and prioritize our peace and well-being over our grievances.

It's also worth noting that forgiveness and release are not linear processes. There will be days when the pain feels fresh, and the idea of letting go seems impossible. That's okay. Healing is not a straight path. It's a series of ebbs and flows of good and hard days. It is essential to keep moving forward, even one small step at a time.

In the end, forgiveness and release are about freeing ourselves to live more fully, love more openly, and embrace the present with all its possibilities. They are about finding peace within ourselves so we can extend that peace to the world around us. And isn't that a journey worth taking?

Embracing Change

Change, they say, is the only constant in life. Yet, for something so consistent, it's remarkably challenging to embrace. Why? Because change nudges us out of our comfort zones, forcing us to confront the unknown. It's like standing at the edge of a cliff, knowing you need to jump but not knowing if you'll fly or fall. But here's the thing about change—it's not just an end but a beginning. It's an opportunity to shed what no longer serves us and to welcome new possibilities. This section is about learning to lean into that leap with open arms.

Imagine for a moment a caterpillar snug in its cocoon. It's a place of comfort, of safety. But it's also a place of transformation. For the caterpillar to become a butterfly, it must embrace the change from within, even if it means leaving behind the only world it's ever known. Like the caterpillar, we are also often cocooned in the familiarity of our routines, relationships, and very identities. And like the caterpillar, we, too, have the potential to emerge transformed.

But how do we begin to embrace change, especially when it feels like a force majeure, an unstoppable wave crashing over us? The first step is acceptance. Accept that change is inevitable, and resisting it only causes more suffering. This doesn't mean you have to like it, but rather that you acknowledge it as part of your reality.

Next, cultivate flexibility. Think of a tree in a storm; the ones that survive aren't the rigid ones that resist the wind but the ones that bend with it. Flexibility allows you to adapt to new circumstances and to learn and grow from them. It's about finding your footing even when the ground shifts beneath you.

And perhaps most importantly, foster a sense of curiosity. Approach change not with fear but with a sense of wonder. What can this change teach you? How can it help you grow? Curiosity transforms the narrative from one of loss to one of learning. It shifts the focus from what you're leaving behind to what you're moving towards.

Of course, embracing change is easier said than done. It's a process, often messy, filled with moments of doubt and fear. But it's also filled with moments of profound growth and unexpected joy. Remember, every butterfly once faced the uncertainty of the cocoon. Yet, it was within that very cocoon that it found its wings.

So, as we navigate the complexities of letting go and moving forward, let's remind ourselves that change, while daunting, is also deeply beautiful. It's the path to discovering new horizons and becoming more resilient, adaptable, and alive. It's about surviving the storm and learning to dance in the rain. And who knows? In embracing change, you might soar to heights you never imagined possible.

Living in the Present

Living in the present is akin to embracing life with both arms wide open, ready to catch whatever comes your way. It's about letting the past be a memory and the future a mystery, focusing instead on the here and now. This concept, simple in its essence, can be incredibly challenging to embody, especially when our minds are cluttered with regrets from yesterday and worries about tomorrow.

Imagine you're walking through a beautiful garden. Still, instead of admiring the vibrant flowers and feeling the sun's warmth, you're glued to your phone, scrolling through old messages or planning your schedule for the next week. This happens when we live anywhere but in the present moment; we miss out on the beauty and richness of life as it unfolds right before our eyes.

The art of letting go teaches us to release the grip on our past disappointments and future anxieties, making room for the present moment to take center stage. It's not about forgetting our past or ignoring the future but acknowledging that the only moment we truly have control over is the one happening right now.

Practicing mindfulness is a powerful tool in this

journey. It's paying full attention to the present moment without judgment. Whether through meditation, deep breathing, or simply being aware of your surroundings and sensations, mindfulness roots you in the here and now, offering peace and clarity amidst life's chaos.

But why is living in the present so crucial? For starters, it enhances your appreciation for life. When fully engaged in the moment, you're more likely to notice and cherish the small joys and wonders you would otherwise overlook. It also reduces stress and anxiety, as many of our worries stem from dwelling on the past or fearing the future. By centering yourself in the present, you're less likely to be overwhelmed by these thoughts and more likely to approach challenges calmly and clearly.

Moreover, living in the present fosters better relationships. Being fully present with loved ones shows them you value and appreciate their company, strengthening your connections. It allows for deeper, more meaningful interactions as you listen and engage with them rather than being distracted by other thoughts.

Embracing the present moment is a journey, one that requires patience, practice, and perseverance. We can all cultivate this skill, leading to a more fulfilling and joyful life. So, take a deep breath, look around, and savor the moment. After all, now is all we really have.

Chapter Summary

- Attachment is a natural human tendency that defines our interactions with people, possessions, beliefs, and experiences. However, it can also lead to suffering.
- Happiness overly dependent on external factors can cause fear of loss, anxiety over change, and pain from separation, overshadowing present joy.
- Letting go involves loosening dependency on external sources for inner peace and happiness and embracing the impermanence of life to reduce suffering.
- Letting go includes acknowledgment, understanding, acceptance, release, and transformation, which guides us toward peace and acceptance.
- Forgiveness and release in personal growth involve acknowledging pain, letting go of resentment, and embracing self-love and future possibilities.
- Embracing change involves acceptance, flexibility, and curiosity, viewing change as an opportunity for growth and transformation.

- Living in the present enhances life appreciation, reduces stress, and fosters better relationships by focusing on the here and now.
- Detachment misunderstood as indifference, is about experiencing life fully without being enslaved by attachments, leading to internal freedom and peace.

12

CREATING YOUR PATH

Vision for the Future

Now, we must cast our eyes forward, envisioning a future that acknowledges the inevitability of suffering and embraces the transformative power of mindset. This vision for the future is not about painting an overly optimistic picture that denies the reality of pain and hardship. Instead, it's about recognizing that within the fabric of suffering lies a profound opportunity for growth, learning, and a more profound sense of fulfillment.

Imagine standing at the edge of a vast landscape, the horizon stretching infinitely before you. This horizon represents the future—endless possibilities of choices, challenges, and chances. The path you choose to walk is uniquely yours, shaped by your experiences, beliefs, and the mindset you cultivate. It's a path that will inevitably traverse valleys of despair and mountains of triumph. Yet, how you navigate this terrain, how you respond to the inevitable suffering, is where your power lies.

The vision for the future I invite you to consider is one where suffering is not a shadow to be avoided but a teacher to be understood. It's a future where the mindset you cultivate—one of resilience, growth, or gratitude—becomes your compass, guiding you through the darkest nights and into the dawn of new beginnings. This vision is not just about surviving; it's about thriving. It's about finding meaning amid chaos and discovering a purpose that propels you forward, even when the road ahead seems uncertain.

To create this path, starting with a foundation of self-awareness is crucial. Understand your values, strengths, and the areas where you seek growth. From this place of understanding, set intentions that align with your deepest desires for the life you wish to lead. These intentions are not just goals to be achieved but beacons to guide your journey, illuminating the steps you take each day.

As you move forward, remember that your mindset is a choice. Choose to see challenges as opportunities for growth. Choose to embrace change rather than resist it. Choose to find joy in the small moments, even amidst suffering. These choices will be challenging, but they are within your control.

Finally, know that you're not alone on this journey. Surround yourself with a community that supports and uplifts you. Lean on others when the path becomes too steep to climb alone. And equally, extend your hand to those struggling to find their way. Together, we can create a future that acknowledges the role of suffering in our lives and celebrates the strength, resilience, and compassion it can foster within us.

Let's hold onto the belief that our paths, though marked by suffering, are filled with infinite potential for transformation and joy. The future is a canvas waiting for us to paint it with the colors of our most profound hopes and dreams. Let's step forward with courage, curiosity, and an open heart, ready to create a path that reflects our deepest aspirations.

Setting Intentions

Setting intentions is akin to drawing a map for a treasure hunt in the journey of life. It's about pinpointing where you want to go, understanding the terrain, and preparing for the unexpected. This process is especially crucial when navigating the complex interplay of mindset and suffering. Intentions act as beacons of light, guiding us through the darkest tunnels and leading us toward personal growth and healing.

Imagine standing at the edge of an expansive desert. The sand dunes are high, and the path needs to be charted. This desert represents the hardships and obstacles we encounter in life. Imagine you have a compass in your hand, with the needle pointing towards your ultimate dreams and goals. That compass is your intention. It doesn't flatten the desert or create a marked route, but it gives you direction, purpose, and the bravery to take the first step.

Setting intentions is more than just wishful thinking. It's a deliberate and powerful act of aligning your heart, mind, and soul with your highest values and goals. It's about declaring to yourself and the universe what truly matters to you and how you respond to life's inevitable challenges.

But how do we set intentions to guide us through suffering and lead to a transformative mindset? It starts with self-reflection. Take a moment to connect with your inner self. Ask yourself what qualities you wish to cultivate, what wounds you need to heal, and what dreams you yearn to chase. This introspection is the foundation of meaningful intentions.

Next, articulate your intentions with clarity and conviction. Use positive, present-tense language that resonates with your core. Instead of saying, "I don't want to feel sad," frame it as "I choose joy and gratitude in my daily life." This positive framing empowers you, turning passive wishes into active commitments.

Remember, setting intentions is not a one-time event. It's a continuous process of recalibration. Your experiences will shape and sometimes change your desires and goals as you journey through life. Regularly revisiting and refining your intentions ensures they align with your evolving self.

Moreover, setting intentions is not just about personal gain. It's about how your journey can contribute to the well-being of others. When we set intentions that include kindness, empathy, and service, we transform our lives and become catalysts for positive change in the world around us.

In essence, setting intentions is about claiming your power to shape your journey through life. It's a declaration that, despite the suffering and challenges you may face, you have the agency to choose your path, cultivate resilience, and pursue a life of meaning and fulfillment. So, take that compass in your hand, set your intentions with heart and courage, and embark on the journey to create your path.

Taking Action

Understanding the landscape of our mindset and the role of suffering is akin to preparing for a long trek in life. We've explored the terrain and equipped ourselves with knowledge, and now, it's time to take the first step. Taking action is not just about movement but the intentional movement toward a unique vision.

Imagine standing at the edge of a vast wheat field. The dense and tall stalks narrate stories of the unknown. This wheat field is your future, filled with furrows that intertwine, lead to clearings, or sometimes culminate in dead ends. The decision to step into the wheat field is yours, and it's profound. It signifies a commitment not just to confront challenges but to rise above them through the power of your mindset.

Taking action means acknowledging that while the furrow may not be straight, the direction is. It's about setting small, achievable goals as stepping stones toward your larger vision. These goals are reference points on your route, guiding you through the wheat field. Each step taken is a testament to your resilience, a muscle that strengthens with use.

But here's the thing about taking action—it's often accompanied by fear—fear of the unknown, fear of failure, and sometimes fear of our own potential. It's natural. Every person who has ever set out to create change has felt it.

The difference lies in how you respond to that fear. Do you let it paralyze you or use it as fuel?

Consider this: every outstanding achievement began with the decision to try. To take that first step despite the fear. Action bridges the world of ideas and the reality of accomplishment. It's bringing your vision to life, one step at a time.

And yes, there will be obstacles. Paths that seemed clear may become overgrown. You might find yourself facing challenges that test your resolve. This is where your mindset, cultivated through understanding and resilience, becomes your compass. It reminds you that suffering is not a roadblock but a part of the journey—a part that has the potential to teach, strengthen, and transform.

Taking action is also about adaptability. It's recognizing when a path leads nowhere and having the courage to backtrack to find another route. It's about being open to the lessons each step teaches you, allowing them to shape your journey in ways you might not have imagined.

So, as you stand at the edge of your wheat field, remember this: taking action is a declaration of hope. It's a statement that says, "I believe in my ability to create change." It's an acknowledgment that while the path may be uncertain, your will to move forward is not.

Your journey through mindset and suffering is uniquely yours. It will be filled with beauty and challenges, clearings, and thickets. But every step you take is towards a future where suffering does not define you—your resilience does. So take that step. Embrace the journey. And remember, the path is created by walking.

The Importance of Patience

In life's journey, especially when navigating through the terrain of mindset and suffering, patience isn't just a virtue—it's a necessity. Imagine patience as the compass that guides us through the stormy seas of our struggles, ensuring we don't lose our way. It's easy to want quick fixes or to see immediate results from our efforts to overcome suffering and foster a healthier mindset. However, the reality is often far from this ideal. The process is gradual, filled with ups and downs, and patience becomes our most trusted ally here.

Let's consider the nature of suffering and the role of mindset in shaping our experiences. Suffering, in its essence, is a universal human experience, one that can profoundly transform us, depending on our approach and perspective. Similarly, our fixed or growth-oriented mindset can significantly influence how we perceive and react to our suffering. The intersection of these two aspects of our lives is where the magic happens, but it doesn't happen overnight. This is where patience comes into play.

Think about the last time you faced a challenge that seemed impossible. Perhaps it was a personal loss, a professional setback, or an internal battle with your thoughts and emotions. The path to overcoming that challenge likely wasn't linear. There were moments when you felt like you had taken two steps forward only to take three steps back. When progress seems invisible, patience whispers to us in these moments, reminding us that growth is happening beneath the surface.

Patience teaches us to embrace the journey, with all its twists and turns, as part of the healing and growth process. It encourages us to look beyond the immediate discomfort and trust the slow, often imperceptible, steps forward. Just as a seed needs time to break through the soil and reach for the sunlight, our efforts to overcome suffering and cultivate a positive mindset need time to take root and flourish.

Moreover, patience allows us to be kind to ourselves. It's a gentle reminder that it's okay to not have all the answers right away and that it's okay to falter as we learn and grow. This kindness, rooted in patience, creates a nurturing environment for our mindset to shift from despair to hope and resilience.

In life, each experience contributes to the larger picture, no matter how insignificant it may seem. Patience helps us see this bigger picture and understand that every moment of suffering and effort to shift our mindset is a valuable part of our journey. It's not about waiting passively for things to get better; it's about actively engaging with our experiences, learning from them, and allowing ourselves the time and space to evolve.

As we continue to create our path, let's carry patience like a lantern, illuminating our way through the darkness. Let it remind us that while the journey may be extended and fraught with challenges, each step forward is a victory in itself, no matter how small. Ultimately, patience transforms our suffering into strength and our mindset into unshakeable resilience.

Celebrating Progress

In life's journey, especially when navigating the rough terrains of mindset and suffering, it's easy to overlook the small victories. Yet, these moments of progress, no matter how minuscule they may seem, are pivotal in shaping our path forward. Celebrating progress isn't just about acknowledging success; it's about recognizing the strength it took to overcome the hurdles that once seemed impossible.

Imagine you're climbing a mountain. The peak is your ultimate goal, but the journey to the top is challenging. Each step forward, each ledge you pull yourself over, is progress. Would you only celebrate once you've reached the summit? Or would you also take a moment, every now and then, to look back and appreciate how far you've come? Celebrating progress is akin to these moments of reflection on the mountain. It's an acknowledgment of your perseverance, resilience, and growth mindset that propels you forward.

Why is celebrating progress so important? For starters, it boosts our morale. When we're in the thick of our struggles, it's easy to feel like we're not making any headway. Taking the time to celebrate the small victories reminds us that we are moving forward, even if it's just one small step at a time. This recognition can be incredibly motivating, pushing us to continue our path with renewed vigor.

Moreover, celebrating progress helps us to reframe our mindset about suffering and challenges. Instead of viewing obstacles as insurmountable barriers, we start to see them as opportunities for growth. Each challenge we overcome is a testament to our strength and resilience. By celebrating these moments, we reinforce a positive mindset that views suffering not as a permanent state but as a temporary phase that we have the power to overcome.

But how do we celebrate progress? It doesn't always have to be grand gestures. Sometimes, it's the simple acts that hold the most meaning. It could be taking a moment to reflect on what you've achieved, sharing your progress with a friend or loved one, or even treating yourself to something small as a reward for your hard work. The key is to acknowledge the effort you've put in and the strides you've made, no matter how small they may seem.

Every step forward is a piece of the puzzle in creating your path in the grand scheme of things. These moments of progress, celebrated and cherished, build the foundation of a resilient and positive mindset. So, as you navigate the complexities of mindset and suffering, remember to pause, reflect, and celebrate your progress. It's not just about reaching the peak; it's about valuing the journey and the lessons learned along the way.

Continuous Growth

Growth isn't a destination; it's a journey. And like any journey, it's continuous, filled with ups and downs, twists and turns. It's about moving forward, even when the path isn't clear, and learning from every step we take. This section is about embracing the idea that growth never stops. It's about understanding that every experience, especially the challenging ones, offers us a chance to learn, adapt, and evolve.

Think of it this way: a tree doesn't grow to a certain height. It grows because that's its nature. It faces storms and droughts; sometimes, it even gets struck by lightning. But it keeps growing, adapting to its environment, and finding ways to thrive. We're not so different. Our growth is also about adapting, learning, and thriving, no matter what life throws our way.

Continuous growth means recognizing that we're never

really "done." There's always something new to learn, a new perspective to consider, or a new challenge to overcome. It's about staying curious and open, even when we feel we've figured it all out. The truth is, the moment we think we have all the answers is when we stop growing.

It also means being kind to ourselves during the process. Growth can be messy, and it's only sometimes linear or pretty. Sometimes, we take two steps forward and one step back, and that's okay. What's important is that we're moving, learning, and not giving up on ourselves.

So, how do we embrace continuous growth? First, we can set intentions that align with our values and what we want to achieve. Then, by taking action, even if it's small steps at a time. And finally, by reflecting on our journey, celebrating our progress, and learning from our experiences.

Remember, growth is not just about reaching a specific goal or milestone. It's about the person we become along the way. It's about building resilience, cultivating a positive mindset, and finding meaning in our experiences. It's about becoming the best version of ourselves, not just for our own sake but for the world around us.

As we close this chapter, let's commit to continuous growth. Let's stay curious, embrace challenges, and keep moving forward. The path of growth is not just about where we're going but who we're becoming along the way.

Chapter Summary

- The vision for the future involves recognizing suffering as an opportunity for growth and fulfillment, not just a challenge to be avoided.
- Envisioning the future as a landscape of possibilities, the path chosen is shaped by individual experiences, beliefs, and mindset.
- Suffering is seen as a teacher, and the mindset cultivated (resilience, growth, gratitude) guides through challenges towards new beginnings.
- Creating a fulfilling path starts with self-awareness, setting intentions aligned with personal values and desires, and choosing a positive mindset.
- The journey is not solitary; community support is crucial for navigating difficult times and fostering strength, resilience, and compassion.
- Setting intentions involves self-reflection, clarity, commitment to personal growth, and contributing positively to others' well-being.
- Taking action toward a vision involves setting small goals, facing fears, and being adaptable to overcome obstacles and learn from the journey.
- Never underestimate the importance of patience, celebrating progress, and continuous

growth as critical elements in navigating life's challenges and fostering a positive mindset.

THE JOURNEY CONTINUES

Reflecting on the Journey

Now, we must pause and reflect on the path we've traversed together. The exploration of mindset and suffering has taken us through varied landscapes of human experience, each chapter a step deeper into understanding the intricate dance between our internal worlds and the external challenges we face.

Our journey began with an invitation to understand the profound impact of our mindset on navigating the inevitable suffering that life presents. We delved into the nature of suffering, not as a distant concept but as a universal experience that connects us all. Through historical perspectives and personal stories, we've seen the many faces of suffering and the resilience of the human spirit.

The exploration of mindset illuminated the power of belief and the reality-shaping force of our thoughts and attitudes. We discovered that a growth mindset isn't just a tool for personal development but a beacon of hope in the darkest times. The chapters on emotions, coping mechanisms, and the power of relationships further enriched our understanding, offering practical insights and strategies to manage emotional pain, build resilience, and foster meaningful connections.

Overcoming obstacles, searching for meaning, and the body-mind connection were not just topics of discussion but invitations to action. Each section equipped us with knowledge and tools to face adversity, find purpose, and nurture our physical and mental well-being.

As we ventured into the science of happiness, resilience in the face of adversity, and the art of letting go, we were reminded that pursuing a fulfilling life is a personal and collective journey. The chapters encouraged us to embrace change, live in the present, and continuously seek growth.

The penultimate chapter about creating your path was a call to action. It urged us to envision our future, set intentions, and take deliberate steps toward realizing our dreams. It reminded us that while the journey is fraught with challenges, each step forward celebrates progress and is a testament to our resilience.

Now, as we reflect on the journey, it's clear that the end of this book is not the conclusion of our exploration but a new beginning. The insights and lessons we've gathered are tools for life, meant to be revisited, refined, and reimagined as we continue to navigate the complexities of mindset and suffering.

The journey continues, and with each step, we are invited to deepen our understanding, expand our capacity for compassion, and cultivate a mindset that embraces the full spectrum of human experience. Let this book be a companion on your journey, a reminder that you are not alone, and a testament to the transformative power of embracing mindset and suffering with courage, curiosity, and compassion.

Staying the Course

As we draw the curtains on this journey, it's crucial to remember that the path ahead is not a straight line. It's filled with twists, turns, and sometimes, steep hills to climb. Staying the course, especially regarding mindset and suffering, is about embracing resilience and maintaining a growth mindset, even when the going gets tough.

Life, in its essence, is unpredictable. We've explored

the depths of suffering and the peaks of mindset shifts that can transform our lives. But knowing and doing are two different things. It's easy to fall back into old patterns, to let the fixed mindset creep back in when challenges arise. That's why staying the course is a commitment and a daily practice.

Imagine you're sailing in the vast sea. Some days, the sea is calm, and the journey feels effortless. On other days, storms rage, and waves threaten to overturn your boat. In those moments, your skill, resilience, and mindset keep you afloat. You learn to navigate the storms not because you're immune to fear but because you've developed the strength to face it.

This journey of understanding mindset and suffering is similar. It's about equipping yourself with the tools and knowledge to navigate life's storms. It's about recognizing that suffering, while an inevitable part of life, doesn't define you. Your response to it does.

Staying the course means reminding yourself of the lessons learned throughout this book. It's about practicing mindfulness, cultivating positive relationships, and embracing change as an opportunity for growth. It's about setting intentions, taking action, and celebrating progress, no matter how small.

But most importantly, it's about patience and kindness towards yourself. Change doesn't happen overnight. There will be days when you feel like you're not making any progress when the weight of suffering feels too heavy to bear. Remember that it's okay to pause, breathe, and take care of yourself in those moments. Resilience is not about pushing through pain at all costs; it's about knowing when to rest and recharge.

As we conclude this journey, remember that the path is yours to create. The lessons in this book are tools in your toolkit, ready to be used when you need them. But the real magic happens when you apply them and make that conscious choice to stay the course, no matter what life throws your way.

So, as you move forward, carry these lessons with you. Let them be your compass, guiding you through the storms and into calmer waters. The journey continues, and so does your growth. Stay the course and trust in the process. The best is yet to come.

Your Feedback Matters

Thank you for joining me on this journey. If the book inspired you, please share your thoughts by leaving a review on Amazon using the QR code below. Your feedback is invaluable and helps guide others. I'm grateful for your time and hope the insights you've gained enrich your quest for knowledge.

ABOUT THE AUTHOR

James Conant is an acclaimed author recognized for his insightful debut book, *"Question Your Truth of Thoughts."* Inspired by personal experiences and extensive research, Conant provides readers with strategies to face life's challenges with resilience. His writing harmoniously blends theoretical exploration and practical advice, offering a roadmap for personal growth and understanding the human condition. Conant's work stands as a beacon of hope, illuminating the transformative power of mindset and resilience, aiming to guide readers through adversity toward a sense of profound well-being.

www.ingramcontent.com/pod-product-compliance
Lightning Source LLC
Chambersburg PA
CBHW052140070526
44585CB00017B/1912